Fostering Girl Child Education in Malawi

Published by
Luviri Press
P/Bag 201 Luwinga
Mzuzu 2

ISBN   978-99960-98-14-7
eISBN   978-99960-98-15-4

The Luviri Press is represented outside Malawi by:
African Books Collective Oxford (order@africanbookscollective.com)

www.mzunipress.blogspot.com
www.africanbookscollective.com

Editorial assistance: Daniel Neumann

Fostering Girl Child Education in Malawi

Cecilia Mzumara

Luviri Press

Mzuzu

2018

Dedication

This book is dedicated to Delia Tetreault, all Missionary Sisters of the Immaculate Conception (MIC Sisters), former, current and future students and staff of Marymount and above all to the Glory of God.

Acknowledgements

This work is a fruit of the encouragement of many people. I am grateful to Mr. Gerry Meuris and St. Luke's Parish of West Island in Montreal (Dollard des Ormeaux), Canada for the moral and financial assistance towards the publication of this book. I am also indebted to the support of my General and Provincial Superiors and their Councils for the funds towards my university studies. I wish to mention Sr. Doris Twyman, my provincial superior from 2007 to 2011. Her simplicity and passion for the youth in many aspects has inspired my own life. Professor Anaklet Phiri, Vice Chancellor of the Catholic University of Malawi, for his trust in my academic efforts and Rev. Professor Joseph Chakanza for his insight and encouragement to publish my thesis as a book.

Worth mentioning are my current provincial superior, Sr. Huguette Ostiguy and all the MIC Sisters in Malawi and Zambia for their intellectual, moral, emotional and spiritual support. I thank Bro. John Katumbi of the Marist Brothers, Fr. Andrew Kaufa and Mr. Charles Kabwaibwai and the entire staff of Montfort Media for their editorial work in shaping my thesis into a book, and to Professor Klaus Fiedler for working on the Print on Demand edition.

Thanks to my brothers and sisters, relatives, nieces and nephews, my teachers, colleagues and friends who have inspired and challenged my life. Particular thanks to my twin Maggie and her family for their humble influence in my life. My dear parents Michael and Elizabeth Chirwa deserve my sincere gratitude for being both parents and educators at their best to their children, grandchildren and many other people whose lives they have touched. My present community of St. Joseph at Marymount in Mzuzu is greatly thanked for their under-standing and time offered for me to complete my work. Much more, for their sisterly love and care, prayer and sacrifices made over the success of this endeavour.

Above all, I thank God for his presence and the abundance of his giftedness in my life. Indeed, like the Psalmist, my heart joyfully acclaims: "From the rising of the sun to its setting, and from the work of this book, may God's name be praised and glorified." May God bless you all with abundant graces.

Sr. Cecilia Mzumara

MIC Sisters

General Introduction

Professor Rev. Fr. Joseph Chakanza of the Catholic University of Malawi (CUNIMA) enjoyed reading through my thesis and making the necessary amendments. Afterwards, he suggested that I publish it. For him, it was a rare opportunity to bring out the contribution of female religious women as regards educational endeavours to the development of the church in Malawi, as well as to the nation as a whole. He felt that this work was part and parcel of Church History with a missiological aspect. Then, I felt that it was also part of my mission to make this contribution known. I came to realize that education is vital to the development of an individual, the Church as well as the nation. In the same manner, Sam Safuli (1998) adds that education equips the individual with knowledge, skills and attitudes that enable him or her to play their roles effectively in an attempt to promote and sustain the socio-economic development of the nation. I took up the challenge with faith and hope knowing that everything is possible for one who has faith (Mark 9:23).

The brief history of Marymount Girls' Secondary School fills my heart with joy. It helps me to appreciate the efforts, risks and challenges which were taken up by my predecessors in the congregation of the Missionary Sisters of the Immaculate Conception (MIC) towards the education of the girl child. By accepting the offer of the Ministry of Education, Science and Technology, MIC Sisters took up the responsibility to start and run Marymount Girls' Secondary School. As expatriate missionaries, they fulfilled their mission work of evangelization. Their foundress, Delia Tetreault often urged her Sisters all over the globe to give a special attention towards the welfare of children, girls and women. As their fellow MIC Sister from the Diocese of Mzuzu, I felt intrigued to discover the immense challenges experienced by the four pioneer MIC Sisters and the others later on, in the establishment and growth of Marymount. The efforts of the Sisters have borne fruit in society through their former as well as the current students of Marymount who keep on "Working with Joy!"

Marymount Secondary School remains a beacon of excellence for the girl child. It reminds me of the Gospel narrative of the encounter between Mary and her cousin Elizabeth in the hill country of Judea (Luke 1:39-45). The meeting of the first MIC Sisters at the "Mount of Mary" in Mzuzu, with the Malawian young ladies was such an encounter of joy. In both the Sisters and the girls, something leapt in their hearts and marked them for the rest of their lives. Through the education received at Marymount, the girls entered a new phase of their personal history. Formal education opened new paths and opportunities to grow into women of dignity at a time when the education of a girl child was not a priority. On the other hand, this encounter also helped MIC Sisters to define their mission and purpose in their evangelization work among the people of Malawi. Hence, the coming in of MIC Sisters enforced the need for parents to educate their girl child with the same intensity as the boy-child. The Catholic nuns were role models who made an outstanding contribution to society although this reality has not been highlighted in both the history of the Catholic Church in Malawi as well as in that of the nation.

It is a fact that the best MSCE results for girls come from boarding secondary schools which were started by female religious congregations. For example, outstanding results come from Marymount, St. Mary's, Likuni, Ludzi Girls', Stella Maris, Our Lady of Wisdom, Nkhamenya and Providence Secondary Schools. I know of many influential women in society who passed through Marymount, other Catholic schools as well as other church related institutions and making meaningful contributions to the socio-economic development of Malawi. In that regard, it is worthwhile to mention that the first female president of our country, Her Excellency Mrs. Joyce Banda, was once a student of Providence Secondary School which is a grant-aided institution under the direction of Catholic nuns, the Servants of the Blessed Virgin Mary (SBVM). Interestingly, she came out in my research work as one of the models for the girls of Marymount. Other influential women include Doctor Muyeriwa and Rosemary Mkanda-wire, chief executive of Toyota Malawi who had been to Marymount, whilst Dr. Mary Shawa, principal secretary in the Ministry of Women and Gender, was at Likuni Girls, a school run by the Teresian Sisters.

On the other hand, many of these schools need expansion and lack both human and material resources to maximize their efforts. These realities cannot be simply accepted. It is an invitation to stakeholders in the field of education to support such endeavors. Similarly, in order to enforce quality education for the girl child, stakeholders could learn from such institutions on how to maintain high standards that would benefit many girls in our secondary schools.

The contents of this book are not exhaustive. However, fifty years later, MIC Sisters and staff of Marymount can look back at their students and marvel at their contribution to the intellectual, spiritual, moral, cultural, social and economic development of their own lives and families, as well as to their churches and Malawi as a whole. Likewise, it invites former and current students to trace their beginnings knowing that their years at Marymount have an impact on what they have become.

As you read through these pages, I invite you to remain grateful to the efforts made by MIC Sisters and religious women of other congregations who work tirelessly for the emancipation of fellow women. Consequently, think of your own way of helping a girl child attain her potential through quality education.

Foreword by Bishop Joseph Mkasa Zuza.

We are pleased to introduce to you a brief history of Marymount Catholic Girls' Secondary School written by one of our own daughters in the Diocese of Mzuzu, Sr. Cecilia Mzumara. The book comes out at an opportune time when we are preparing to celebrate the Golden Jubilee of Marymount. In January 2013, Marymount clocks fifty years. This indeed is an occasion for the Diocese of Mzuzu, Marymount Catholic Girls' Secondary School and all students and staff to appreciate the contribution the school have made to the Diocese of Mzuzu and the country as a whole.

When talking about Marymount, you cannot avoid talking about the Missionary Sisters of the Immaculate Conception, popularly known as MIC Sisters. They were asked by Bishop Jean Louis Jobidon to take care of the school and provide quality education to the girl child. We are grateful to them for having assisted the Diocese in this apostolate.

Marymount Catholic Girls' Secondary School was a grant-aided school, but in 1992 negotiations started with the Government of Malawi to have the school privatized. It is in the same year that the Catholic Bishop's issued their pastoral letter entitled "LIVING OUR FAITH". In the same year, my predecessor, Monsignor John Vincent Roche, who had initiated the idea of the privatization of Marymount, was deported from Malawi. This, however, did not stop us from privatizing Marymount. We believe that both as a grant-aided and now a Catholic private school, Marymount has been providing quality education to the Malawian girl child.

Through this brief history of Marymount, we hope the readers will be made aware that the MIC Sisters were the first female Missionary Congregation who came to the Diocese of Mzuzu. They spread throughout the whole Diocese of Mzuzu which included the present Diocese of Karonga. The MIC Sisters together with the Missionaries of Africa, popularly known as White Fathers, led the foundation of the work of evangelization. The Sisters were involved in education, health, pastoral, youths and women development. Their help to Monsignor Marcel St. Denis and later on to Bishop Jean Louis Jobidon cannot be over-emphasized.

One of the fruits of their apostolate is the founding of the Sisters of the Holy Rosary, our own local congregation which has now taken over most of the institutions that were established by the MIC Sisters.

We are therefore very grateful to all MIC Sisters who have served in the Diocese of Mzuzu since 1948. Many have passed on to eternity and for them we pray that they may Rest in Peace. Others have retired and are in their home countries and we say to them, have a good rest for the job well done. We still have a few expatriate missionary Sisters and we say to them, keep it up. We have a growing number of Malawian MIC Sisters as well as Sisters from other African countries. To them we say keep the fire burning, follow the footsteps of your predecessors.

This book which gives a brief history of Marymount Catholic Girls' Secondary School should inspire us that quality education requires selflessness and hard work as demonstrated by the early missionaries. Quality education also requires discipline which Marymount has and continues to give to the girl child. It is our hope that both former and current students of Marymount will, by reading this book, be inspired to reflect and look back at what Marymount has done for them. Yes, Marymount has made you who you are today. Our appeal to you is that you should be good ambassadors of Marymount and when possible contribute something to your school.

We would like to congratulate Sr. Cecilia Mzumara for writing this book. May every reader be inspired by the work of the MIC Sisters who offered their lives in helping others through offering quality education. Remember, we are all called to be the light and salt of the earth. There-fore, as Jesus teaches us: *Your light must shine in people's sight, so that, seeing your good works, they may give praise to your Father in Heaven* (Matthew 5:16). Let us all be good ambassadors of Marymount.

+Right Rev. Joseph Mkasa Zuza

Bishop of the Diocese of Mzuzu

6th May, 2012.

Foreword by Sr. Huguette Ostiguy MIC

In January 1963, the Missionary Sisters of the Immaculate Conception (MIC Sisters) welcomed seventy Malawian girls to the newly erected Marymount Girls' Secondary School in Mzuzu. This was in response to the dream of the late Right Rev. Monsignor Marcel St. Denis, first administrator of the Catholic Diocese of Mzuzu. He desired to have a girls' secondary school beside Chaminade of Karonga which was for boys only. This was the first step in the realization of a big dream: helping young women to acquire secondary education that was needed to participate more fully in the social and economic development of Malawi and to exercise fruitfully their Christian leadership. His dream was realized by his predecessor, the late Right Rev. Bishop Lewis Jobidon, first bishop of Mzuzu Diocese.

This journey is 50 years old now and as we celebrate the Golden Jubilee of Marymount Catholic Girls' Secondary School, we want to acknowledge the special contribution of the school to the development of the girl child in Malawi and to the role played by the MIC Sisters, teachers and ex-students. Special acknowledgement to women who in one way or the other, at times in silence, but nevertheless important, who have contributed to the progress of the society at large and for Christianity in particular.

The school has faced different challenges over those fifty years, but the dedication to offer quality education to girls has overcome all difficulties and the school has moved forward and continues to be where excellence is seen not only through the academic results of the students, but also in the quality of their participation in social issues of the country.

Sr. Cecilia Mzumara, a member of the young African MIC Sisters, took up the challenges of analyzing and presenting to the public the achievements of Marymount Secondary School towards the girl child education in Malawi. This page of history is worth remembering as it has set the stages for thousands of women who have and still hold positions of influence in different spheres of the society and in their churches.

We thank you sincerely, Sr. Cecilia Mzumara, for the hard work which allowed you to write this page of history in a very lively style and for the courage to present this story to the public. It is a treasure of information for everyone, for those who spent some years at

Marymount either as a student, teacher or support staff, and also for all of us who know about Marymount without knowing the whole story of commitment and dedication which has built and kept Marymount alive over the years.

A final word of thanks to everyone who contributed to the life of Marymount, especially to all the students who made Marymount a school where 'Work with Joy' has always been a reality which brought forth fruits of excellence.

Sr. Huguette Ostiguy MIC

Provincial Superior

Our Lady of Africa Province of Malawi and Zambia

8th December, 2012.

ABBREVIATIONS AND ACRONYMS

ACEM	Association of Christian Educators in Malawi2
AIDS	Acquired Immuno-Deficiency Syndrome
Bro.	Brother
CCAP	Church of Central African Presbyterian
CDSS	Community Day Secondary School
CHAM	Christian Hospitals Association of Malawi
CUEA	Catholic University of East Africa
CUNIMA	Catholic University of Malawi
CUSO	Canadian Union of Social Order
ECM	Episcopal Conference of Malawi
EFA	Education for All
FPE	Free Primary Education
Hill	Henry Henderson Institute
HIV	Human Immunodeficiency Virus
INSET	In-service Training
MANEB	Malawi National Examinations Board
MCP	Malawi Congress Party
MDGs	Millennium Development Goals
MHRRC	Malawi Human Rights Resource Centre
MIC	Missionary Sisters of the Immaculate Conception
MISS.Africa	Missionaries of Africa
MOEST	Ministry of Education, Science and Technology
MMM	Medical Missionaries of Mary
MSCE	Malawi School Certificate of Education
MSOLA	Missionary Sisters of Our Lady of Africa
MZUNI	Mzuzu University
PIF	Policy and Investment Framework
PTA	Parent Teacher Association
RC	Roman Catholic
SHR	Sisters of the Holy Rosary
SNE	Special Needs Education
Sr.	Sister
UDHR	Universal Declaration of Human Rights
UN	United Nations
UNICEF	United Nations Children's Emergency Fund
UNIMA	University of Malawi
VSO	Voluntary Services Overseas
WF	White Father
YCS	Young Christian Students

Contents

Foreword by Bishop Joseph Mkasa Zuza.   9

Foreword by Sr. Huguette Ostiguy MIC   11

Chapter One:
Introduction   17

Chapter Two:
The Missionary Sisters of the Immaculate Conception   21

Chapter Three:
Establishment of Marymount Secondary School   31

Chapter Four:
From Grant-Aided to Private   54

Chapter Five:
Marymount 2000 - 2010   64

Chapter Six:
The Specific Contribution of MIC Sisters to Girl Child Education   76

Chapter: Seven:
Suggestions and Recommendations   94

Bibliography   103

Chapter One
Introduction

The modern missionary movement that affected the African continent was an enterprise of both men and women alike, but the contribution of women to formal education was overshadowed by the prowess of their male counterparts.[1] Consequently, their endeavour was not recognized in its own right. Pope John Paul II stated that women are ready and willing to give themselves generously to others, especially in serving the weakest and most defenseless.[2] In whatever they do, women exhibit a kind of affective, cultural and spiritual motherhood, which has inestimable value for the development of individuals and the future of society.[3]

Various sectors of society, the Church and State and the progress of all humanity are deeply indebted to the contribution of women. However, throughout the ages, humankind has been conditioned by a history that has been an obstacle to the progress of women. As such, women's dignity has often been unacknowledged and their prerogatives misrepresented and often relegated to the margins of society, where women have even been reduced to servitude.[4] This has prevented women from truly being themselves and has resulted in a spiritual impoverishment of

---

[1] John Baur, *2000 Years of Christianity in Africa: An African Church History*, Nairobi: Paulines, 1998, p. 409.

[2] John Paul II, *Letter to Women. Presented on the Eve of the Fourth World Conference in Beijing: 4th — 15th September, 1995,* Balaka: Montfort, 1995, p. 10.

[3] Ibid.

[4] Ibid, p. 4.

humanity.[5] Nevertheless, the work of women religious towards the emancipation of fellow women in Malawi cannot remain under cover.

The Christian Church has had a long history of involvement in the education of women and girls.[6] Learning was preserved and promoted in monasteries of both male and female orders at the time when the general population was illiterate.[7] Formal education in Malawi came with the arrival of active apostolic orders of missionaries in the late 19th century. As a basic human right, education has been recognized since the 1948 adoption of the Universal Declaration of Human Rights (UDHR).[8] It is in the same year that the Missionary Sisters of the Immaculate Conception (MIC Sisters) came to Malawi from Quebec in Canada, upon invitation by the Missionaries of Africa (White Fathers). The Sisters first arrived at Katete Mission in the Prefecture of North Nyasa and immediately took charge of the girls' boarding primary school and of the health centre. During the school session of 1955-1956, a girls' private secondary school was opened at Katete, but eventually moved to Karonga as St. Mary's Secondary School which was a mixed school.[9]

Later, the school moved to Mzuzu as Marymount Girls' Secondary School, which was officially opened in January 1963. The boys moved to Chaminade, which was under the Marianist Brothers. A few years earlier, the Catholic Bishops of Nyasaland had issued a pastoral letter, "How to Build a Happy Nation" dated 20th March, 1961.[10] The Catholic Church, like other early missionary churches, realized that the key to building a happy nation on the eve of independence was through education. The Church had numerous primary, secondary and technical schools. The Catholic nuns did much for the education of girls. By

---

[5]   Ibid.

[6]   Dr Suzanne Scorsone, "The Church has defended women's rights for 2000 years." On behalf of the Holy See. 42nd UN Commission on the Status of Women in 1998. http://church_empowers_women.html [24.4.2010].

[7]   Ibid.

[8]   Ibid.

[9]   Dayire Kumwenda, Saint Theresa Catholic Parish, Katete: Origins. Growth and Development (1938-2005), BA, University of Malawi, 2005, p. 8.

[10]   "Joint Pastoral Letter of the Catholic Bishops of Nyasaland, 20.3.1961. Lessons from History. 'How to Build a Happy Nation'," 1-12, no. 42, Balaka: Montfort, July-August 2003.

1968, the Church had seven girls' grant-aided boarding secondary schools under the direction of religious nuns of various congregations.[11]

This book outlines the contribution of the Missionary Sisters of the Immaculate Conception (MIC Sisters) towards girl child education in Malawi with particular focus on the establishment, growth and development of Marymount Girls' Secondary School in Mzuzu, from 1963 to 2010. The appraisal by former students of Marymount, reveals the courage of the pioneering Sisters towards the empowerment of fellow women in places where they were sent to evangelize in spite of numerous challenges that they encountered in the process. The history of Marymount shows that education of the girl child provides a viable means to development and improvement of life at family, nation and world level.

The Church as well as the State consider education as key to the achievement of the Millennium Development Goals (MDGs). It shows that a school is a global entity of its own kind which ensures practical living of the goals at basic level and in the process, shaping people for the future. In Malawi, it is shown that girls perform best in single-sex boarding schools, particularly those started by missionary groups under the Roman Catholic Church, which offer adequate resources and a conducive environment for meaningful and lasting education. This noble task is reflected in the high levels of success that girls' boarding schools such as Marymount have achieved since their inception. Women who have passed through such schools have excelled in life and continue to contribute meaningfully to the country's development in many aspects.

Most male-led groups in the Roman Catholic Church focused on evangelization through catechizing and recruiting converts. However, they found themselves in a culture where, being men, it was

---

[11] In the Southern Region, St Mary' in Zomba and Our Lady of Wisdom Private Secondary School in Limbe are under the Daughters of Wisdom. Stella Mans is under the Sisters of Our Lady. In Mulanje, Providence is administered by Sisters of the Blessed Virgin Mary (SBVM). In the central region, Likuni Girls is run by Teresian Sisters, while Ludzi Girls is under the Sisters of Charity of Ottawa (SCO). In the Diocese of Mzuzu, Nkhamenya Girls and Kaseye are run by the Sisters of the Holy Rosary (SHR). There are many others which have mushroomed in the recent past like Bakhita Secondary School in Balaka under the Canossian Sisters.

customarily difficult to reach out to women directly. The question of how to meaningfully contact women and girls brought in the presence of female religious congregations to complete the ministry of the missions. It is this form of evangelization that most female-led groups embraced. They immediately took charge of schools, health centres and women affairs to the greatv relief of the male groups thus raising the human spirit by giving both training and opportunity for fulfilment in areas relating to education, labour and economic rights.[12]

Recent studies in Malawi show that girls are more disadvantaged than boys in accessing quality education.[13] On the other hand, women religious congregations in the Roman Catholic Church have, for a long time, invested both human and material resources in the promotion of girl child education, but there is scanty information of that contribution. Likewise, there is very little in-depth case studies on girls' secondary schools in Malawi hence denying their contribution and a wider scope of knowledge to the people of Malawi. Realizing that aspect, this work has been conducted to narrow that gap, reveal and appreciate such contribution in a systematic manner as it impacts on girls themselves as well as on the people and nation as a whole.

Girl child education in Malawi cannot be fully achieved by a multiplicity of mixed secondary schools but by a deliberate effort to enforce single-sex boarding schools. Women Religious Congregations in the Roman Catholic Church take an active role in the education of the girl child.

---

[12] http://www.its.cattech.edu/women-cp/churchempowermenswomen [24.4.2010].

[13] Action Aid Malawi, *The Existence and Implementation of Laws, Policies, and Regulations in Education and how they Affect the Girl child in Malawi,* Lilongwe, undated, p. 8; Bridget Manda, Impediments to the Girl Child's Realization of the Right to Access Basic Education in Malawi: The Case of Chintheche Area in Nkhata Bay District, MA, Mzuzu University, 2015.

Chapter Two
The Missionary Sisters
of the Immaculate Conception

The Missionary Sisters of the Immaculate Conception (MIC Sisters) were founded in 1902 at Montreal, in Quebec Province of Canada. Their foundress, Delia Tetreault, was born on 4th February, 1865. Her mother died when she was only two years old and she grew up with foster parents who were childless.[14] They gave her good formal and Christian education. In her time, Quebec had numerous religious congregations founded by the Catholic missionaries from France. Many women congregations worked in the fields of education, health and social welfare. With growing pastoral needs, Delia started an Apostolic School to train girls for missionary work.

Delia at 18 years   Delia as MIC

The school soon turned into a missionary congregation under the patronage of the Blessed Virgin Mary, hence the name Missionary Sisters of the Immaculate Conception given by Pope Pius X.[15] It became the first female missionary institute of Canadian origin with the aim of proclaiming joyfully the Good News of Salvation in Jesus Christ.[16] As early as 1909, Delia sent her first group of sisters to China.

---

[14] The young sister of her mother, Julie and her husband Jean Alix adopted Delia.

[15] G. Barrette, *Delia Tetrault and the Canadian Church*, Laval: MIC Mission Press, 1989, p. 14.

[16] *The Constitutions of the Missionary Sisters of the Immaculate Conception,*

Such an evangelizing spirit led to the opening of different mission houses both in Canada and abroad.

MIC Sisters on the African Continent

Monsignor Marcel St. Denis

The presence of MIC Sisters in Africa is a continuation of the zeal and audacity of Delia Tetreault. In 1894, she desired to come to Zimbabwe for missionary work, but fell very ill just before her departure. She did not realize her dream in her lifetime but kept desiring that one day her missionaries would open up missions in Africa. Meanwhile, evangelization on the African continent was blooming through various French congregations like the Missionaries of Africa founded by Cardinal Lavigerie. He opened several missions in West Africa and was well-known for his fight against slave trade in the Sub-Sahara.[17] Back in Montreal, the laity in MIC retreat houses had learnt of the African Continent from travelling missionary priests, especially of the White Fathers. Many young ladies who experienced such moments of spiritual renewal got attracted to missionary life and joined the MIC Congregation. Missionary life was very challenging during the Second World War from 1939 to 1945. Soon after the war, MIC Sisters opened houses in Haiti, Cuba and South America. At about the same time, the Sacred Congregation for the Propagation of the Faith in Rome asked the MIC Sisters to come to Africa, either to Cameroon or Nyasaland. In July 1947, the Apostolic Prefecture of Northern Nyasaland was established by Rome. Its Prefect, Monsignor J. Marcel St. Denis, a Canadian Missionary of Africa, (WF) appealed to the MIC Sisters inviting them to come to Nyasaland. This was the third invitation after Fr. Albert of the Sacred Heart Fathers in Foumban, Cameroon and Monsignor J.M. Blomjous Apostolic Vicar of Maswa in Tanganyika (Tanzania) in May 1946 and February 1947 respectively. Monsignor St. Denis met the MIC Superiors at the Generalate in

---

5.1, 1983, p. 33.

[17] Dayire Kumwenda, Saint Theresa Catholic Parish, Katete: Origins. Growth and Development (1938-2005), BA, University of Malawi, 2005, p. 3.

person. The Sisters opted for Malawi, then Nyasaland and another group of sisters left for the Island of Madagascar three years later. It is worth noting that there was a general movement towards missionary activity within the Roman Catholic Church inspired by the Catholic Action in the early 1900s.[18] This movement started in Europe and spread through to North and South America. It stressed the need for individual commitment to spread the Kingdom of God. It was largely responsible for the presence of Catholic missionary activity that found its way into the African Continent.[2]

MIC Sisters in Nyasaland (Malawi)

Sr. Madeleine Loranger

The first four Canadian MIC Sisters: Madeleine Loranger, Berengere Cadieux, Paul-Ida Coulombe and Therese Gouin left Montreal by train to New York in the United States of America. From New York, the Sisters boarded a warship that took them around Cape Town in South Africa to Beira. From there they travelled by train to Malawi.[19] Their entire journey took close to one month before arriving at their destination: Katete Mission in Mzimba District. They were welcomed by Msgr. St. Denis on 19th May, 1948 at his headquarters at Katete which was the first Catholic Mission in the north of Nyasaland. It had previously been an outstation of Chiphaso under the Likuni Vicariate.[20] A few months later, the pioneer sisters were followed by six other companions: Alice Pepin, Marie-Marthe Therien, Yvette Ricard, Annette Corbeil, Bernadette Fyfe and Marie-Claire Lacombe.[21]

---

[18] Ibid.

[19] Response to questionnaire via email from Sr Marie-Claire Lacombe, MIC.

[20] A Vicariate is a juridical mission area not yet under a bishop but designated to become a Diocese.

[21] Marie-Claire Lacombe and Berengere Cadieux are still alive and retired in Laval, Canada. At the age of 89 years Sr. Marie-Claire responded to the entire questionnaire.

In a territory dominated by Scottish Missionaries, the White Fathers were regarded as intruders. However, Monsignor St. Denis targeted places that were not yet in close range of the Scottish missions. The Monsignor had worked in the British navy as chapterlain during the Second World War. He knew the mind of the British authorities such that it was not difficult for him to win the favour of the British in their colony of Nyasaland.[22] It is appreciable that the Scottish Missionaries under the Livingstonia Mission spearheaded educational endeavours in the north of Malawi. The Overtoun Institution was quite famous since 1895.[23] The centre boasted of a girls' school and another one for the blind as some of the institutions at Khondowe.[24] However, promotion of girls and women education was largely pronounced with the coming in of the Roman Catholic Mission in the region. Monsignor St. Denis had in mind "the promotion of education for both boys and girls, especially the girls."[25] With his successor Bishop Jobidon, they had at hand a larger group of religious missionaries both male and female to advance their diverse activities as compared to their Scottish counter-parts. The latter were mainly pastors with their families and had to assume most of the activities at central mission stations. Many schools in the rural areas were opened upon the arrival of three Catholic missionary groups namely the White Fathers, Marianist Brothers and the MIC Sisters. Their celibate vocation helped them to fully dedicate their lives without divided responsibility between family roles and their work of evangelization. They also came in large numbers to intensify their common mission.

---

[22] Interview with Sr Huguette Pigeon, MIC. She worked at Marymount in the 1960s. She was diocesan auditor for many years. She is still alive and an active member of CADECOM in Mzuzu Diocese. During the Second World War, the Canadian army was an ally of the British and many priests served as chaplains in different camps.

[23] For a local perspective, see: Happy Nyambose, The Establishment and Contribution of the Overtoun Institute in Northern Malawi and Beyond (1895-2010), MA, Mzuzu University, 2015

[24] John S. Munthali, The Role of the Livingstonia Synod in the Promotion of Girls' Secondary Education, BA, University of Malawi, 2005, p. 5.

[25] Typed notes found in MIC Chronicles of Marymount Convent; Interview with Sr Huguette Pigeon, MIC.

MIC Sisters' Sectors of Evangelization

As soon as MIC Sisters arrived at any mission, three major activities of evangelization took place. Schools, health centres and women groups were established. Between 1941 and 1966, they were fully operational. Nyasaland was a mission land and various activities were starting for the first time.

Primary Schools

Upon arrival at Katete, Sisters Madeleine Loranger and Berengere Cardieux organized a boarding house for 8 girls. Out of 114 pupils in the mixed school opened by the Missionaries of Africa, only 15 were girls.[26] Those facilities were the foundation of Katete Girls' boarding primary school. In 1949, a convent was opened in Rumphi where sisters taught at the primary school. In 1951, St. Mary's in Karonga and Kaseye girls' primary school in Chitipa were opened. From 1952 to 1956, the MICs run a primary school at Vua, near Chilumba in Karonga district.

Sr. Berengere Carddieux

The parish at Vua had to be closed due to the rising level of the Lake Nyasa. Eventually, the mission was submerged. A year later, the sisters opened St. Maria Gorretti in Nkhata-Bay where a remarkable growth in girl child education took place. For a total of 150 boys registered at the opening of classes in 1953, there were only two girls. Sr. Yvette Belanger moved from house to house to talk to parents about the importance of sending their daughters to school. In 1962, the school enrolled 320 girls from grades one to eight.[27] In other primary schools like St. Paul's at Mzimba Boma and Mzambazi in Euthini area, the Sisters taught at mixed schools for both boys and girls. In the late 1980s MIC Sisters accommodated the girls with physical disabilities who accessed primary education at St. Paul's.

Teacher Training Centre

The White Fathers ran a mixed Teacher Training College at Katete called St. John Bosco which was opened in 1948. A good number of

---

[26] *Precursor*, 75th Anniversary Issue no. 4, 1977, p. 9.

[27] *Precursor*, 75th Anniversary Issue no. 4, 1977, p. 9.

girls who successfully completed their primary course were immediately enrolled for teacher-training as vernacular grade teachers for two years. The MIC Sisters were part of the teaching staff such as Sr. Imelda Saurette and Sr. Gabrielle Saucier. In 1952, Miss Barbara Moore, the Education Inspector of the Northern Region, gave the vernacular grade examination to the first four students. Successful young ladies included Rufina Moyo, Victoria Kamanga, Elizabeth Chirwa and Catherine Zuza from Katete.[28]

Health Centres

Amongst MIC Sisters were some with medical skills. Health Centres were built at the central mission where the sisters got established. This preceded any health facilities offered by government. The sisters' main focus was on good health of mothers and children. Sisters Yvette Caron, Pauline Longtin, Yvette Carle, Louise Lefebvre, Louise Denis, Jeanne d'Arc Corriveau and Jacqueline Vachet are among those who worked for many years in dispensaries and clinics.

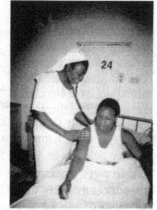

Sr. Anastazia Manda, a young MIC nurse with a patient

In Mzimba, the sisters operated a mobile clinic under the direction of Sisters Gertrude Pare and Colette Leclerc.[29] The sisters emphasized good child-care and proper nutrition. Their interaction with mothers was essential in insisting on education of their children as soon as the child had reached school-going age.

---

[28] Response to questionnaire sent to Sr Marie-Claire Lacombe. Rufina and Victoria became sisters of the Holy Rosary whilst Elizabeth and Catherine became teachers and dedicated mothers, leading stable and well founded Christian families. Elizabeth is the daughter of Ignacio Chirwa, first catechist of Katete Mission.

[29] The Malawi Government took charge of the health centre and built Mzimba Hospital and some rural clinics. The sisters did not want duplication of services and withdrew. Most health centres are still operational under the direction of the Sisters of the Holy Rosary at Katete, Mzambazi, Rumphi and Kaseye.

Women Promotion

The Sisters quickly established craft centres for women in all their mission stations. The focus was on teaching women how to read and write, for those who had dropped out of primary school or those who never went to school. They also taught housecraft, sewing, knitting, and cooking. For nursing mothers, the Sisters took the occasions to teach them good nutrition, health care and home management. Sisters Edith Faucher, Laurette Gauvin, Jeannette Fanfan and Marie-Therese Katongo, worked for many years for alphabetization at Delia Centre in Mzimba and other surrounding places.

The Foundation of the Sisters of the Holy Rosary

In 1951, Msgr. St. Denis founded the first diocesan congregation for women in Mzuzu Diocese. The first group of Sisters of the Holy Rosary (SHR) received their formation under the guidance of MIC Sisters, especially Sister Madeleine Loranger, one of the MIC pioneers and Sr. Bernadette Dumas. The assistance of the MIC towards the local congregation was one way of promoting

Sisters of the Holy Rosary

women in church and society. Many of the Sisters were former students in MIC schools. Most of the work in schools and hospitals were later handed over to the Sisters of the Holy Rosary. This signifies the growth of the local Church and ensured continuity of the missions and opening of new sectors of evangelization.

Challenges Encountered by the Pioneering Sisters

Language

Many Sisters who came in the 1940s up to the 1970s were French Canadians. Communication among themselves was in French. Some of them knew both English and

Chinese, Malawian, Canadian and Philippina MIC sisters

27

French, either before coming for mission or they perfected it during their studies. At school, the sisters communicated in English as the official language. The sisters who worked in hospitals and parishes learnt Chitumbuka much faster than those who went directly to schools because they had the opportunity to practice it.[30]

Weather

For many Sisters, the tropical weather was quite different from the freezing North American climate. They found the rainy season humid and the worst was the cold of June and July, especially at Katete and Mzuzu without any heating system. On the other hand, the heat along the lake especially in Karonga and Nkhata-Bay was scorching for most missionaries. A good number of them served for a few years and could not adapt themselves due to malaria which forced them to return home. However, the zealous spirit never stopped others to come over and take their place.

Adaptation to Food

In the late 1950s and 60s, the missionaries had difficulties to find foodstuffs appealing to their taste. The Sisters were used in their home-land to store food for over six months during winter. In Malawi they felt that sense of insecurity and had difficulties to preserve food as they lacked fridges. At times they had meat when a Brother was lucky to hunt for a deer and that served a big feast for the whole community.[31]

Communication

It was difficult for the missionaries to commute from one mission centre to the other. Often, they would send men on bicycles for emergency messages. The Sisters would cycle to outstations during weekends for various apostolic activities. Long trips were organized to combine several activities at school, parish and health centres. Each mission station had only one car to service all the needs of their scattered population. Besides, there were no tarred roads anywhere in

---

[30] Pioneer Sisters of Katete recall the selfless help of Catechist Ignacio Chirwa and his wife Cecilia Phiri and their children and neighbours who assisted them in learning the language.

[31] The sisters appreciated local foods such as maize, porridge, bananas, sweet potatoes and a variety of seasonal fruits.

the North at this stage. Trips from Mzimba to Mzuzu would take five or more hours and those to Blantyre would take two to three days.

Culture

It is the Sisters who introduced boarding facilities for girls in catholic mission schools. This was a revolution in the mentality of the local people in the North and in the entire country where education of the girl child was not valued in the same manner as that of the boy. sending girls to school meant delaying their founding a family that was traditionally dictated by society. The concept of *lobola* was another factor that pushed parents to marry their daughter off early.[32] The practice facilitated the marriage of the girl's brother or brothers who could use the same herd to bring in-laws in the village.

The girls who chose to become religious sisters met resistance from their parents and relatives. Religious life was a new phenomenon for the people. For many people, the cultural beliefs that a woman was meant to get married and bear children was still strong.[33] A childless woman was regarded as eternally infant, and an unmarried woman was a disgrace to society. However, many girls found out that the missionaries lived a meaningful and happy life in their celibacy and dedicated their lives to serve others.

Conclusion

This chapter has traced the coming of the MIC Sisters to Nyasaland and the various activities that they embraced. The Sisters soon felt that they had many things to do in a new diocese where they were the first and only female congregation at the time. In order to ensure expansion, meaningful evangelization and development in the Church and State,

---

[32] *Lobola* is the bride price of the boy's family in a patriarchal system. It is predominant in the northern part of Malawi and some parts of Lower Shire. In the former days when almost every household had a kraal, about 5-7 cows were asked for *lobola*. Today, the bride price is paid in monetary form, not necessarily to the equivalent of cows' value.

[33] In an interview with an ex-student and former teacher of Marymount, Sr Leonia Moyo, SHR, she said that some girls could not cope with boarding school life, which was foreign to them. The girls loved the free village life without timetable for class, work and play as the Sisters organized it with dictates of the formal education.

education was to be prioritized. The Sisters put a strong emphasis on girl child education to attain their desired goal of promoting the lives of women and the entire community. The next chapter explains the establishment, growth and development of Marymount Girls' Secondary School.

Chapter Three
Establishment of Marymount Secondary School

The increase of pupils in primary schools run by MIC Sisters demanded more teachers. Similarly, a pressing need was felt for young African men and women in education and health, alongside missionary staff. Many youths got employed after completion of grade six of primary education. Others went for teacher training courses in various colleges. The abolishment of Church-run primary teacher training colleges increased the desire for completion of secondary school studies. This prompted MIC Sisters to look beyond primary education for the girls. This chapter will focus on the establishment, growth and development of Marymount Girls' Secondary School.

The Pioneering Stage: 1956-1973

The history of Marymount begins much earlier than the actual date of foundation. Monsignor St. Denis chose Mzuzu as his future residence and he had at heart to establish there a hospital and a girls' secondary school.[34] He asked for plots in Mzuzu but he was told by the Colonial Administration that no plots were to be sold unless the whole Limphasa Project land in Nkhata-Bay was sold. He soon found money to buy the land. After this development, the colonial administration allowed Monsignor St. Denis to buy plots in Mzuzu. In order to have the European population on his side, he accepted their request to have a

---

[34] The development of Mzuzu started in 1955 with a tung estate, and when the tung oil prices dropped on the world market, it was made the administrative centre of the Northern Region. See Zeenah Sibande, *The Religious Geography of Mzuzu City in Northern Malawi*, Mzuzu: Luviri Press, 2018.

convent primary school for the education of their children at Marymount.[35]

Justification of a Girls' Secondary School.

In 1954, a private secondary school for girls was opened at Katete. It started with four girls. This was the first time in Catholic history to have a girls' secondary school in the North. The school flourished quickly. By 1956, five girls were brought to Karonga on St. Mary's grounds and by 1959 they were 20 in number.[36] Karonga secondary school was co-educational. Quite soon, the school needed renovation and expansion since it was accommodating both primary and secondary school pupils. It

Bishop Jean Louis Jobidon

was then decided that a boys' secondary school and a separate girls' secondary school would be built in the diocese of Mzuzu. The decision was further enforced after the British Government offered a substantial grant to the Catholic Mission after insistent pleas by Msgr. St. Denis. He left the prefecture in 1957 due to illness and his dream was pursued by his successor Bishop Jean Louis Jobidon. The boys' school moved from down the lake at St. Mary's to *Bwiba* and was renamed Chaminade. The girls' school was to be built in Mzuzu and named Marymount.

This separation was symbolic of initiation rites from a cultural perspective where after puberty, boys and girls lived in their houses called 'mphala' and 'nthanganeni' respectively. This was a mark of adult living preparing the youths for an independent life later on. Education was perceived in a similar manner. An education aimed at a girl child had a mission to fulfill and Marymount was well-placed and well-timed. This would help the girls to concentrate on their studies and excel, protecting them from domination by the boys. This was not a

---

[35] Typed notes of Sr Jacqueline Bastien, first headmistress of Marymount, undated, found in the chronicles of the 1960s.

[36] *Precursor*, 75th Anniversary, Issue no. 4, 1977, p. 9.

deliberate move by missionaries to cut off the youth from their cultures as some critics of mission education tend to believe.

The move also echoes the single-sex education policy for secondary education that exists in the Catholic Church at local and universal level. On the other hand, it was evident that independence from the colonial rule was inevitable in the late 1950s and early 1960s. The missionaries foresaw that prominent women and men would be needed in leadership roles in church and state and in the private sector. The school's objective was to develop to the maximum the aptitudes and potential of the girls at all levels including arts and sports.[37]

Construction of Marymount

True to her letter of 19th March 1960, Miss Moore, the Education Inspector for the North, visited the Sisters to inspect the proposed site for the construction of the school. After lengthy deliberations, satisfaction was reached and permission was granted to have the plans drawn. The MIC Superior, Sr. Beatrice Tessier, requested more Sisters from Canada for Nyasaland. Bishop Jobidon asked Mr. R. Pugh, an architect to prepare the plans that were to be submitted to the government. Bro. Jean-Marie was asked to take up the project as contractor under the Diocese of Mzuzu.

Funding

MIC Sisters

The Sisters' major role was to ask for donations to realize the project. They applied to various donors as well as their headquarters in Canada to assist. Shortage of water was one of the major difficulties that the pioneer Sisters faced because Marymount was built on a plateau. The first purchase was a water pump and engine. Through the active supervision of Sr. Berengere Cadieux, the ground had been leveled, the roadway planned and the bricks fired.[38] The Sisters kept records and reported the expenses accordingly. They gave the Brothers of the Missionaries of Africa the entire contract to build the school as funds

---

[37] *Precursor*, 75th Anniversary, Issue no. 4, 1977, p. 10.

[38] Sr Berengere, one of the pioneer sisters to Malawi, was well known as Amayi Yosefe. She is now living in the home of the elderly Sisters at Port-Viau in Canada.

permitted them. By 1961, the first stage of construction was completed which comprised of one dormitory, two classrooms, a biology room, a staff-room, a dining-room and a kitchen.[39] The renovation and extension of the Convent and building of the School Chapel were solely from the Sister's own funding.

The Diocese

Financially, the Diocese of Mzuzu relied on MIC Sisters, donors and government grants to build the school after initiating the idea. A few Brothers of the Missionaries of Africa worked at the construction of Marymount. Other Brothers who replaced Bro. Jean-Marie were Bro. Booman and Bro. Joe Eberle. Fr. de Repentigny did the difficult job of levelling the grounds of Marymount. The numerous beautiful terraces and flowers one can admire today are the result of his incessant toil. It is recorded that Fr. de Repentigny began leveling the sports grounds in February 1963 with the help of two workers with their shovels and wheelbarrows.[40] Later, a Mr. Mdyawomba from Mzuzu Welfare Centre obtained a tractor from the government to help him. In March 1964, Mr. G. Merril, Chief sportsman, arrived at Marymount with a bulldozer sent by the Malawi Government and UNESCO to prepare the sportsground.[41] Other contributions to help in improving school buildings and premises came from church organizations like the Christian Service Committee. In the late 1980s, Sr. Denise Duhamel reworked the landscaping giving Marymount its present appearance.

Beit Trust

Beit Trust was a big donor towards the infrastructure at Marymount. In recent years, the Trust has built a hostel that has facilitated the expansion of boarding facilities at the school. Buildings such as the library, science laboratory, and home economics block were built

---

[39] Sr Gisèle Leduc, Marymount in Retrospect 1963-1973, undated.

[40] Ibid, p. 3.

[41] In an interview (August 2010) Sr Huguette Pigeon and Sr Yvonne Ayotte told me that this was a wonderful error as the tractor was meant for Mzuzu Government Secondary School which was also headed by an expatriate headmaster, Sir Martin Roseveare. After three weeks at Marymount, the driver was asked to withdraw but the leveling was quite advanced so that permission was granted to complete the work.

between 1967 and 1971. In September 1970, Mr. Rilly was sent by government to see the construction. In March of 1972, Sir Robert Armitage and Mr. J. Ingham, representatives of Beit Trust in Rhodesia, visited the school. They were particularly interested in the construction of the Administration block which they had just funded. In 1974, the Trust gave MK 6,000.00 for its extension.[42]

The Malawi Government

The Colonial Government gave the first grant to construct Marymount. In 1967, the government of Dr. Hastings Kamuzu Banda funded the extension of the hall which was the biggest in town. Important social and political functions scheduled for the North, like the Malawi Congress Party Conventions, were held at Marymount. In 1979, the ministry of education gave MK 12,000.00 to help in the construction of the fence around the school. This was after a visit by the education minister where the students requested for the facility.[43] The government was responsible for selection of pupils and payments of salaries of teachers on government scale. All expatriate teachers were receiving fixed allowances from government which were far from adequate.[44]

Dr. Hastings Kamuzu Banda, first president of Malawi.

---

[42] MIC Chronicles, 6.3.1972.

[43] MIC Chronicles, 6.2.1979.

[44] In an interview with some of the Sisters, one said, "The sisters worked very hard; they had more responsibilities than the other teachers, but they were receiving less." Another Sister said, "I never found this really 'fair' because the Sisters were numerous at that time and they were careful in budgeting and spending. This was to help the diocese. The diocese was poor at that time." In a similar context, around 1960s, the diocese asked the MIC Sisters to buy all their convents in which they resided, to help the diocese.

Campbell Trust, Misereor and the Canadian High Commission

In 1978, the school received MK 11,000.00 from Campbell Trust for the construction of a new laboratory. The new building was meant to cater for the teaching of agriculture. It was a second donation from Campbell after MK 14,850 was given for the construction of a library. Misereor, a German organization, donated MK 5,000.00 for class equipment and materials.

By April 1986, Brother Joe Eberle had begun the construction of a new wing to the school kitchen to house six electric pots that had been acquired through financial help obtained from the Canadian High Commission. This greatly improved the preparation and quality of meals offered to the boarders. The school started a double stream in 1967 and by 1978, it had over 360 boarders.[45]

The Development of Marymount

Marymount was officially opened on 29th January 1963 with forms one, two and three. It had registered seventy students and had four teachers, all MICs. Form one students were

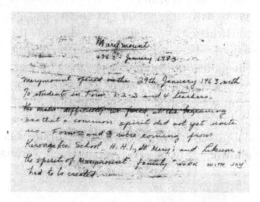

Handwriting of Sr. Jacqueline Bastien

Sr. Jacqueline Bastien
MIC

selected from various primary schools throughout the country. The girls in form two and three came from Karonga Secondary School, Henry Henderson Institute in Blantyre (HHI), St. Mary's in Zomba and Likuni in Lilongwe.[46] The first headmistress was Sr. Jacqueline Bastien who came with her stu-

---

[45] MIC Chronicles, 6.2.1978; also of 21.4.1986.

[46] Sr Gisèle Leduc, Marymount in Retrospect 1963-1973, undated, p. 1.

dents from St. Mary's in Karonga. The other three teachers were Sisters Suzanne Rinfret, Helene Labelle, and Doris Twyman. The Sisters chose "Work with Joy" as the motto of the school.[47] The official blessing of the school was done by Bishop Jobidon on 25th July 1964 amidst over 140 invited guests from Church and government circles.

Chaplaincy

It was the desire of the Sisters to have a Chaplain to assist them in serving the spiritual needs of the school and promote Christian formation and character building among students. The Sisters combined their roles as Christian educators and evangelizers. The first chaplain of Marymount was Fr. Marcel de Repentigny from 1963 to 1972. Apart from the spiritual care of the Sisters, students and teachers, he helped with the construction of the school and paid school fees for needy students. Other chaplains at Marymount after him were Fr. O'Leary, Fr. J. Coolen, Fr. Langlade and currently Fr. Jim McGuire, a Scaboro missionary.[48]

The Sisters and chaplains interacted well amongst themselves as evidenced at some social gatherings. In the early 70s, there were many Protestant missionaries in Mzuzu. From such cordial relationships, the Sisters found out some volunteers for Marymount. For instance, in 1979, Mrs Caroline Swafford volunteered to teach at Marymount which experienced some shortage of staff. She was the wife of an American Baptist Minister in Mzuzu. She taught for a few months without any payment.[49]

---

[47] The emblem of the school was designed by Sr Doris Twyman. She taught for 25 years at Marymount. Until the time of this research, she was the Provincial of the MIC Sister, Malawi and Zambia.

[48] Many who studied at Marymount from 1973-1987 have great memories of Fr L'Heureux, who died just before his 75th birthday, while serving as chaplain to Catholic students at Mzuzu Government Secondary School which was a mixed school, opened in 1959. All chaplains were Missionaries of Africa (White Fathers) while Fr Jim is a Scabboro Missionary.

[49] Gary and Caroline Swafford, together with Njolomole Phiri, established the first Baptist Church in Mzuzu in 1972 (Hany Longwe, *Christians by Grace - Baptists by Choice. A History of the Baptist Convention of Malawi*, Mzuzu: Mzuni Press, 2011, pp. 77-81.

The School Library

The Sisters ensured that the library was one of the first buildings to be erected at Marymount. It was stocked with a variety of books to assist both the teachers and students in the process of teaching and learning. Educational

Marymount students in the library

visits at the school were incomplete without a visit to the library. The Sisters, other missionaries, the British Council and the French Consulate donated good and relevant books to the school. Every year, there was special time allotted to the form ones for initiation into the best use of the library. In the process, the Sisters found out that appreciation for reading was not part of the girls' upbringing. Instead of taking a story book to read, most girls were rushing for photo-albums to admire the lives of their predecessors.[50]

Academic Programmes

At inception, Marymount ceased to be a private diocesan secondary school as it was at Katete and Karonga. It became a grant-aided secondary school and followed the government curriculum for secondary schools. A variety of subjects were taught. These were Commercial Studies, Chichewa, Biology, Bible Knowledge, English, French, Geography, History, Physical Science, Mathematics and Integrated Courses. The latter included Home Economics, Needle Craft and Typing. At the end of form four, students wrote Cambridge School Certificate Examinations from England. These examinations stopped in 1972 when the Ministry of Education introduced the Malawi Certificate of Education Examinations (M.C.E.)

---

[50] MIC Chronicles, 13.10.1970 and 20.1.1971. One nun commented that the girls preferred to look at photos of their friends than to reading a book. It was a gradual process for them to get interest in reading for knowledge, relaxation and study.

Teachers and their Roles

The first Malawian teacher to come to Marymount was a Mr. Kumwenda in 1965, a Malawi Young Pioneer (MYP) who taught agriculture and physical education. The small number of teachers kept increasing as the school progressed. In September 1967, a new group of expatriate teachers included Miss. L. Harris, from Voluntary Services Overseas (VSO) in England,

Sr. Victoria Chirwa and members of staff in 1973

Miss E. Razia, from Canadian Union of Social Order (CUSO), Sir Martin Roseveare,[51] Madame Jacqueline Lavoie and a couple, Mr. and Mrs. R. Perrone, as lay missionaries.[52] By 1973 the school had 22 staff members, twelve of them MIC Sisters. By then Sr. Victoria Chirwa was Acting Headmistress. Her deputy was Sr. Yvonne Ayotte who was at the same time head of the English department. Sister Therese Blais taught commercial studies whilst Marie Leclair taught English and Bible Knowledge. The head of the Mathematics department was Sr. Marie-Claire Lacombe.[53] Sr. Suzanne Rinfret taught Geography and Sr. Elizabeth Gagne took on Biology and Mathematics. Sisters Doris Twyman and Huguette Pigeon taught Home Craft. Sr. Librada Bantilan was the first Phillipina Sister at Marymount and taught Physical Science. A former Marymount student, Sr. Franciska Moyo of the Sisters of the Holy Rosary (SHR), taught History.

Amongst other expatriates from USA and Canada, were Mr. and Mrs. W.H. Pawek from Los Angeles who were heads of Physical Science and Biology respectively. Miss Margo Shirkie taught English whilst Mr. Denis Sobeck taught French.[54] The lay Malawian teachers included

---

[51] See: *Joys, Jobs and Jaunts. Memoirs of Sir Martin Roseveare*, 1984.

[52] After his retirement from Mzuzu Government Secondary School, Sir Martin Roseveare came to teach at Marymount. He was also a very active member of the school board.

[53] A lot of information for this research was obtained via her email messages.

[54] There were many expatriate teachers at Marymount including Mr David Suley from the USA and his wife from the Philippines also came; Japanese

Mrs. D.C. Phiri who taught Chichewa and Physical Science. Mr. A.G. Hara taught Agriculture and Physical Education as MYP teacher. Mr. J.W. Nhlema was the laboratory assistant. The Sisters on the support-staff were Bernadette Dumas and Celine Laurin who were bursar and matron respectively. Sister Huguette Ostiguy replaced Sr. Celine Laurin from 1979 to 1988 as matron, bursar, driver, and sister-in-charge of the school dispensary. In the first ten years of existence, over thirty-five Sisters worked at Marymount at different levels.[55]

Mr and Mrs W. Pawek

Extra-Curricular Activities

The Sisters believed in wholistic education and supported it as much as they could. Sharing some of their own talents and skills was as important as imparting knowledge in a classroom. A variety of activities were introduced to supplement academic work which was already well founded. Every teacher was involved in an extra-curricular activity of one form or another. This led to a friendly relationship between teachers and students which created a conducive environment for meaningful learning. The 'Marymount Panorama of 1973-1974,' gives a clear insight into the nature of the activities which were offered to the students in the first ten years of the school's existence.

The Merry Band

The Merry Band began in 1964 under the direction of Sr. Francoise Saucier. She started the band with a dozen recorders and two accordions. The sisters were accustomed to music in their own schools back in Canada. In 1966, Sr. Denise Duhamel, who had the keenest interest in music, made rapid progress in the formation of Merry Band. She was able "to play a surprising number of instruments and what is more, was most enthusiastic about sharing her musical knowledge with

---

volunteers who served for a period of two years; Miss Canada in the 1980s.
[55] MIC Chronicles — records from 1963 to 1973.

the girls."[56] From their home leave, Sisters Denise Duhamel and Jacqueline Bastien would always come back to Marymount with a few musical instruments. These included trumpets and clarinets. At the occasion of an evening concert on 10th August 1970, the German Ambassador, Mr. Berdard Heichback, enriched the band with a gift of an electric guitar, a baritone, a French horn and a clarinet.[57] This was a second gift to the band after having donated two saxophones and two trumpets for the school. The twenty members of the band had at their disposal other instruments such as clarinets, trombones, drums and cymbals.

The band played a variety of music consisting of marches, waltzes, rhumbas and Christmas Carols. It entertained visitors like school inspectors, ministers, foreign dignitaries, religious and political leaders. On public gatherings such as Martyrs Day on 3rd March, Youth Week closing ceremonies, and independence celebrations, Merry Band played the National Anthem in town. The band continued as long as Sr. Denise was at Marymount. She was not replaced after her posting back to Canada. Marymount students who lived during the era of the Merry Band have fond memories and bemoan its demise.

Merry Band

The Snapshooters Club

Photography is a skill that has developed with growing technology. Marymount girls were privileged to learn various skills of photography very early in life with the assistance of Mr. W. Pawek. The club was started in 1969 with four students from each class. They learnt how to

---

[56] Report of one meber of Merry Band in *Marymount Panorama*, vol 11, 1973-74, p. 8. Sr Denise told me that before joining sisterhood, she was a member of a family band, which owned a music firm. The family, which included her parents, brothers, sister and a few cousins travelled to various places giving concerts. She taught a few young MIC Sisters some line dances in 1995, when she came back to Africa, but was later posted to Kanyanga Mission Hospital in Lundazi, administered by the MIC Sisters.

[57] Sr Gisèle Leduc, Marymount in Retrospect 1963-1973, undated, p. 4.

snap, develop and print nega-
tives in the dark room. The
chairlady of the group kept
the camera. A small fee was
charged for individual photos. It was enough to buy
equipment and take a yearly
excursion to interesting places like Nkhatabay and the

Snapshooters Club

Nyika National Park. These visits helped girls to appreciate the beauty
of our beautiful Land of Malawi and its natural resources.

The Red Cross Club

The Red Cross Club was a likely
off-shoot of the Girl Guides that
were introduced at Katete in
1952 by Sr. Gabrielle Saucier.
This group was approved by
Mrs. Watson from England.[58]
The girl-guides' influenced the
girls' education, helping them to
develop a sense of honour and
duty to serve God and their
country. Under the guidance of
Sr. Suzanne Rinfret, the girls

The Red Cross Club

also received various lectures on hygiene, health and on the signs of
various ailments. The students enjoyed most the practical First Aid
lessons as they practiced on each other various methods of tying
bandages. This skill was helpful during school athletic competitions
and during public functions in town. At such occasions, Marymount
Red Cross Club was always invited to be amongst the First Aid Service
Providers.

The Typing Club

Sister Therese Blais was very devoted to the typing club. The girls
found typing very enjoyable. One club member noted that the first
lessons were very difficult for most girls who had never touched a

---

58 Interview with Sr Huguette Pigeon, MIC, Mzimba, 7.9.2010.

typewriter. The school had about 40 typewriters and the students were introduced to "Pitman's Business Typewriting."[59] The club enforced the theories in the commercial class. For many girls, the certificate earned them secretarial work after their form four examinations. With the high demand of such work in

The Typing Club

government departments, companies, and the private sector, typing was an asset for students who took up this course.

The School Magazine

The first school magazine called *"The Effort"* came off the press at the end of 1963.[60] Other publications had various titles such as *'Marymount Smiles,' Marymount Calling,' The Echo'* and special publications like *Marymount in Retrospect'* which marked the tenth anniversary of the school. It was followed by *'Marymount Panorama'* which was centered on clubs, giving a general idea of the importance of extracurricular activities in school.[61] The magazine spurred the creativity of its young contributors. The girls were always proud to bring a copy of their school magazine to their parents and relatives. Currently, the school magazine has adopted the title; *The Echo'* and is published every month.

Handiwork, Knitting and Home-Economics Clubs

The handiwork, knitting and home economics clubs were very popular and most attractive to the girls. Sisters Huguette Pigeon and

Home Economics Club

[59] Hilda Banda, in *Marymount Panorama*, 1973-1974, vol 11, p. 17.

[60] Sr Gisèle Leduc, Marymount in Retrospect 1963-1973, undated, p. 6.

[61] It would have been very difficult for me to write about clubs, if Sr Doris Twyman had not offered this small magazine.

Doris Twyman took charge of club 1 and 2 respectively. The students appreciated the sisters for the chance of knowing home economics which they felt was an important course for them. Students were introduced to various recipes in cookery lessons as well as different patterns in sewing classes. In 1973, a National Conference of domestic science teachers and inspectors of both primary and secondary schools was held in Zomba. Sr. Huguette Pigeon represented Marymount female teachers at that occasion. Dr. Hastings Kamuzu Banda was very keen in supporting domestic sciences and graced that conference by his presence.[62]

Darts Game Club

Sports and Athletics

Netball Team

The students were introduced to a variety of sportive activities like netball, volleyball and athletics. From the very beginning, the Sisters saw the link between a healthy body and a healthy mind. However, this way of thinking was not familiar to the girls. The Sisters had to convince the students to love sports and benefit from it by their own example. After having observed some reluctance, a few Sunday afternoons in September 1964, a team of Sisters would go to the playing field for an hour of netball.[63]

With such lived example, the attendance for sports soared. Amongst the many devoted and enthusiastic sports coaches at Marymount were Sisters Hélène Labelle and Françoise Saucier. The list also includes lay

---

[62] Interview with Sr Huguette Pigeon. She gave the original photo of that day, which she had kept for many years as one good souvenir as a domestic science teacher.

[63] MIC Chronicles, 13.9.1964.

teachers like Mr. Schimth, Miss Ellen Super and Miss Penny Wright. Marymount girls were represented in several regional, national and international competitions. Other clubs included the French Club, Marymount Choir and Guitar Club, The White and Blue Drama Club as well as the In-Door Games' Club with its popular darts game.

Other Social Activities at Marymount

Fashion Shows

The first Marymount fashion show took place at Mzuzu social hall on 24th November 1963. Marymount fashion shows were very unique in that girls wore dresses sewn by themselves. On such occasions, needlework articles were displayed all round the room. After examination of displays and the fashion show itself, judges selected the best pieces of work and prizes were awarded. At the first show, Honourable Q. Chibambo gave out the prizes. The shows were held yearly until 1969. Afterwards, the socio-political context of the time contributed to the discontinuation of fashion shows. The shows were politicized and confused with the beauty contest shows in districts, regions and at national level.

Youth Week

The introduction of Youth Week in 1965 by Dr. H. Kamuzu Banda was a noble cause for the developing nation. He felt that this was one way to form the youths at an earlier stage to do voluntary work which demanded generosity and self-giving. It fostered a spirit of patriotism and love of the country where the young people participated in its young development. The social impact it had was likened to principles found in a paper entitled *"Education for Self-Reliance"* by the late Mwalimu Julius Nyerere, former President of Tanzania. He was one of Africa's respected statesmen and a famous education reformer. Nyerere initiated change in curricula, school organization and students' life in such a way that education meant sharing of resources produced by people's efforts.[64] Consequently, schools and local communities participated voluntarily in various developmental projects. This cultivated a spirit of hard work, acquisition of manual skills, pride in one's labour and love for a clean environment.

---

[64] G.A. Bennars, J.E. Otiende & R. Boisvert (eds), *Theory and Practice of Education*, Nairobi: East African Educational, 1994, pp. 23-24.

Christian Service Week

The Christian Service Week was organized by the Ecumenical Christian Committee under the Christian Service Committee.[65] Every year in November, the committee set aside one week to remind Christians of their duty towards their neighbours, especially to the the needy. At Marymount, the Sisters organized the week with the students and involved prefects to prepare various charitable activities for the elderly, the sick, poor families with orphans and the widows in the neighbourhood. Besides manual work, the students contributed various items like money, bars of soap, packets of salt, sugar and pieces of cloth. In that way, the school helped the girls to be sensitive and compassionate to the needy living around them. At the same time, the girls were helped to integrate work and prayer for the common good.[66]

Christian Organizations

The Young Christian Students (YCS)

The Sisters introduced the YCS group as early as 1963. YCS was organized in order to promote Catholic Action among the students. This movement was very popular after the Second Vatican Council in many Catholic institutions like parishes, schools and colleges. At Marymount, YCS and other Christian movements were mostly founded and supported by Sr. Doris Twyman. The Catholic Action method of 'SEE-JUDGE-ACT' was adopted in the YCS meetings in 1966. The method encouraged students to criticaly thinking about different aspects of their Christian life. It brought to light an awareness of social and moral issues like teasing, theft, abortions and relationships. It promoted practical skills in leadership and communication. It also enhanced good character, moral and spiritual formation of students. Several

---

[65] The Christian Service Committee was an ecumenical faith-based organization, which was active in 1980s. It ran various activities to uplift the human and spiritual lives of people. Most of the activities were in rural areas, especially education and health sectors. The Committee has evolved and has various branches under Christian Council of Malawi and Episcopal Conference of Malawi, such as ACEM, CHAM.

[66] *Ora et labora* (pray and work) was the motto of St Ignatius of Loyola, founder of the Jesuit Society. The Sisters were influenced by this diction for it translated well the attitude of two of the influential ladies in the Gospel: Mary and Martha (Lk. 10:38-42).

46

Marymount girls were elected to regional and national YCS Executive Teams as early as 1970.[67]

The Students' Christian Organisation (SCO)

The Students' Christian Organisation was for all denominations. It aimed at deepening the spiritual life of students through prayer and the study of the Holy Scriptures. The movement was introduced at Marymount by Reverend Whitehead, a Presbyterian Minister. It also had senior friends like Sr. Yvonne Ayotte, Sr. Therese Blais and Mrs. S. Kachale. Both YCS and SCO held similar activities that included Bible study, drama, debates, inquiries and Bible sharing.[68] These groups also did charitable work towards the needy, especially at the hospital, with the aged in the neighbourhood and with the prisoners. Joint meetings with other branches were also held within and outside Marymount. The formation of spiritual groups in schools within Mzuzu and other parts of the diocese was through the initiative of the MIC Sisters.

Prominent Visitors to Marymount

In the first phase of the establishment of the school, various groups of visitors came to Marymount. They ranged from local leaders, school inspectors, ministers of education, resource persons, religious and political leaders. These visits exposed the girls to the sociopolitical and religious atmosphere of Malawi at the time. Consequently, the

Sr. Yvonne Ayotte with SCO members

speeches given by educationists and local leaders encouraged the girls to work hard and contribute effectively to the life of the country. The visitors also had a good picture of what a girl child can become once

---

[67] Catherine Fulculani was in the national team. By 1973 she was in the USA for further studies.

[68] Inquiries were practical case studies related to students' life, especially in the YCS meetings. It is through the inquiry that students applied the "See - Judge - Act" Method.

empowered with secondary education. The visits left a mark on the growth of the school and the fame of Marymount.

Ministry Officials and Education Ministers

Between 1975 and 1979, Marymount was visited by Hon. R.T.C. Munyenyembe, E.B. Muluzi,[69] Justin Malewezi and Dick Matenje in their capacity as Ministers of Education. In his visit, Mr. Matenje requested the form fours of 1979, not to hesitate to apply for TTC as there were 4,000 vacant places in Malawi's primary schools. He also reminded students of their luck to receive their education at Marymount with teachers who were dedicated to their work.[70] As one of the first girls' schools to be established, it could have given the government and some other churches some impetus to establish their own girls' secon-

Dr. Bakili Muluzi once Minister of Education, became Malawi's first democratic president

dary schools on the same model. For instance, Lilongwe Girls Boarding Secondary School is the only secondary school owned by government specifically for girls. It was opened in 1963. Similarly, the Synod of Livingstonia did not feel threatened by the establishment of Marymount. The Synod opened Ekwendeni Girls Secondary School, some 25 km away, only in 1975.[71]

---

[69] Bakali Muluzi became the first president of Malawi in the multi-party democracy in 1994 under the United Democratic Front (UDF); Malawezi served as vice president.

[70] MIC Chronicles, 9.5.1979.

[71] Interview with Sr Yvonne Ayotte. The MIC sisters were asked to open Ekwendeni Girls Secondary School. The Sisters and Bishop Jobidon refused the offer in the mid 1970s because they felt that they already had difficulties to run Marymount in terms of personnel and payments for high land rates and

In the colonial era, the synod ran a girls' secondary school at Ekwendeni but it was closed and moved to Khondowe.[72] The Catholic Church alone had already seven girls' grant-aided secondary schools in Malawi by 1968.[73] Perhaps this explains the satisfaction of government with education offered by religious Sisters in mission girls' schools that it did not pre-occupy itself further in opening more schools for girls. Instead it opened more co-educational institutions like community day secondary schools.

Foreign Dignitaries

Marymount was exposed to a variety of foreign dignitaries. This was unique in the history of secondary schools. Such interaction encouraged the girls in their education. In 1968 the British High Commissioner with over 100 guests visited Marymount. In 1969, the President of Madagascar, Mr. Tsiranana and his wife came to Marymount. In 1970, three dignitaries visited Marymount in April, May and August. These were the French Ambassador Mr. J. Nouvel and his wife; also, Madam Burshett, wife of the American Ambassador, and the German Ambassador Mr. Bernhard Heibach and his family.

Exposure to Political Functions

Sisters, students and teachers of Marymount witnessed the birth of the nation in 1964, under the Malawi Congress Party. At midnight of the 5th of July 1964, the flag was mounted to announce the dawn of Independence. This was followed by a Thanksgiving Eucharistic Celebration in the chapel by Bishop Jobidon. A week later, official celebrations were held in Mzuzu. Marymount students participated in the sportive activities. Marymount hosted the Malawi Congress Party conventions every three years from 1967 until 1988. The venue changed when Mzuzu Teachers' College was built as it was more

---

taxes. – It is Livingstonia Snod's explicit policy to promote girls only secondary school to address gender imbalances (Oswald Jimmy Banda, The Enhancement of Girls Education in CCAP Synod of Livingstonia, MA module, Mzuzu University, 2008.

[72] John S. Munthali, The Role of the Livingstonia Synod in the Promotion of Girls' Secondary Education, BA, University of Malawi, 2005, p. 8.

[73] Kelvin Banda, A *Brief History of Education in Malawi,* Blantyre: Dzuka, 1982, pp. 14-15.

spacious. However, party functions like conventions and crop inspection tours of the president had their own pressures on teachers as well as on the education of girls. Crop inspection tours were the most disturbing because they took place during the rainy season where travelling was difficult and risky in the muddy roads. It is in one of such trips to Karonga that girls had an accident and one girl from Marymount and another from Euthini Secondary School got killed. That accident, in 1987, left many others wounded.

Women and girls were forced to dance at rallies that often took place during school time.[74] Although some girls enjoyed such type of adventure, others soon got tired of it and saw its effects on their lives. It affected their performance in the end because teachers could not finish their syllabi and students were less prepared for final examinations.

The Consolidation Period (1973-1992)

The first ten years of Marymount's existence were crucial in setting up the foundation of the school. The next 19 years saw to the growth and expansion of its programmes in various aspects. Within this time-frame, over 1,580 girls finished their form four. Consequently, the school started to reap the fruits of her labour through former students who returned to Marymount from various universities overseas and from within Malawi as teachers and administrators of the school. Unlike in the first ten years where the majority of teachers were Sisters, this period saw more lay teachers than Sisters. The numbers of Sisters started going down even though a new generation of Sisters came to Marymount to replace pioneering sisters, among them, a few Asian and African Missionaries.[75]

Beacon of Hope

Marymount became a beacon of hope for other girls' schools. Educational visits from within and outside Malawi intensified. A group of 20 head teachers of Primary and Secondary schools from South Africa, in Lesotho and Johannesburg visited Marymount. Likewise,

---

[74] E. Mkamanga, *Suffering in Silence: Malawi Women's 30 Year Dance with Dr. Banda,* Glasgow: Dudu Nsomba, 2000, 55.

[75] Amongst the African Sisters were Sisters Jacintha Henry (a Tanzanian teacher), Pascalina Mpundu and Imelda Katongo (Zambian students who helped in pastoral needs of the school).

three sisters of the Congregation of the Missionary Sisters of Our Lady of Africa (MSOLA) visited the school to learn about administration and some teaching methods used at Marymount.

Similarly, Marymount gave the Sisters of the Holy Rosary quality experience of how to run their own girls' secondary school. After teaching at Marymount for several years, former students like Sisters Leonia Moyo and Mary Kaunda administered Nkhamenya Girls' Secondary School which was handed over to them from the Missionary Sisters of Our Lady of Africa (MSOLA).

Change in School Administration

For the Sisters, the biggest change in the administration of the school came in 1983. By this time, the government directive to replace expatriate teachers with Malawians was already in effect. MIC Sisters did not have any Malawian Sisters in their Congregation until 1996.[76] As such, their only hope was to recommend one amongst their former students.

Mrs. Matilda Kaluluma Kabuye was already deputy headmistress from 1981. She became the first lay headmistress, taking over from Sr. Yvonne Ayotte. From then onwards, MIC Sisters assisted in the administration of the school as members of the board of governors, deputy head teachers and support staff.

Sr. Doris Twyman with Mrs. M. Kabuye

During the consolidation period, the school also faced challenges. Two major challenges were finances and the loss of some members of staff due to posting of well qualified

---

[76] The first Malawian Sister to join the MIC and reach final commitment is Sr Charity Zimba. According to tradition of the Sisters in the diocese, Monsignor St Denis and Bishop Jobidon had requested the MICs not to recruit early for their congregations to give chance to the local congregation of the Sisters of the Holy Rosary to take root. This was a good decision, but it had serious consequences on the MICs, for it created a big gap and somehow made it difficult for them to continue most of their noble works in the diocese due to lack of personnel.

teachers to other schools. Financially, government grants were not always adequate and often not in time for the effective management of the school. The Sisters were very creative and relied on other projects to keep the school running.

New Apostolic Endeavours

The changes in the administration of the school also reflected on MIC personnel in the diocese. The Sisters assumed various other activities in the administration of the congregation at both provincial and international level of the institute.[77] Others ventured into new avenues due to the social realities of the time.

Sr. Cecilia Mzumara with youths

As soon as Malawi publicly declared about the emergence of HIV and AIDS, the Sisters felt that they needed to be equipped in order to assist the students better. HIV and AIDS is a pandemic that would curb the lives of vulnerable youths if serious educational measures were not put in place. The presence of more Malawian teachers at Marymount also allowed some Sisters to concentrate more on Christian and moral formation of students' lives. This strengthened their efforts in YCS and Anti-AIDS Clubs.[78]

Social Participation

Marymount intensified its social activities and solidarity with the local community. For instance, the year 1981 was a year for people with disabilities. A big walk was organized in Mzuzu. Some Sisters and 30

---

[77] Sr Gisèle became the General Bursar and went back to Canada and returned 12 years later. Sr Victoria was a missionary in Cuba and Peru. Sr Yvonne became the Provincial Superior but remained in the board of Marymount. Sr Jacqueline became Secretary of the Provincial Superior and came back to Marymount as Librarian at one point.

[78] Education for Life Experience is the program of Youth Alive Malawi. It tackles various issues that put youth at risk of getting HIV virus. Some issues critically studied are making choices, sexuality and spirituality, cultural aspects and HIV/AIDS, abstinence and effects of contraceptives.

Marymount girls took part in a 16 km walk.[79] In the same year, Marymount sent a representative to the Commonwealth exchange programmegramme to the United Kingdom for three weeks. Maida Nyirongo was the only lady representative from Malawi. The other three were college boys. It was reported that there were only two females in that conference which had groups from the Bahamas, Barbados, Botswana, Kenya, Lesotho, Mauritius, Swaziland, Trinidad and Tobago and Zambia.[80]

The Catholic Church in Mzuzu

The changes in the administration of the diocese had impact on Marymount Girls Secondary School. In 1987, Bishop Jobidon returned to Canada due to poor health which was also aggravated by his advanced age. He was replaced by Monsignor John Roche, an Irish Missionary of St. Patrick's Society. He was a joyful and dynamic pastor, full of new vision for the running of the diocese. Like his predecessors, Monsignor Roche was supportive of the Sisters' efforts towards various programmes to enhance girls' education. He also shared other plans about his perception of Catholic Education in his Diocese which led to the change of the status of Marymount from a grant-aided institution to a Private Catholic Secondary School.

Conclusion

This chapter has dealt with the establishment of Marymount Secondary School. The funding and actual construction of the school was a result of collaboration of different stakeholders in government, donor communities, the diocese, and among the Sisters themselves.

The various academic and extracurricular programmes laid the foundation o the school and made Marymount a unique educational institution. Visits were also influential in motivating girls to work hard. The consolidation period between 1973 and 1992 sealed the programmes which were set up in the school and pointed towards future orientations. Major challenges were in the finances, changes in the administration of the school and within the diocese. The latter leads us to the fourth chapter which will focus on the transition of Marymount from being a grant-aided institution, to a Catholic Private Secondary School.

---

[79] MIC Chronicles, 1981.
[80] MIC Chronicles, July 1981.

Chapter Four
From Grant-Aided to Private

The dream to privatize Marymount was progressive in the heart and mind of Diocesan authorities, especially of Monsignor John Roche, who was the Apostolic Administrator of Mzuzu diocese from 1988 to 1995.[81] Apparently, all mission schools were reckoned diocesan institutions since 1964 and religious congregations were mere agents of those institutions.[82] This chapter will focus on the factors that led to the transition process as well as on objectives of the private school. It will further discuss the roles of the three main partners in the process, namely; the Diocese of Mzuzu, the

Monsignor John Roche

MIC Sisters, and the Government through the Ministry of Education, Science and Technology.

Factors for Privatization

Complaints by the Lay Faithful

Many lay faithful were complaining that their children were not selected to Catholic grant aided schools like Marymount and Nkhamenya Girls, in Mzuzu Diocese. These complaints were made

---

[81] On 6.5.1995, the Vicar General Fr Joseph Mukasa Zuza became the first local bishop of Mzuzu Diocese.

[82] Questionnaire response of Sr Yvonne Ayotte, MIC. Sr Yvonne was the last MIC headmistress and she worked for many years as chairperson of the board of Marymount.

known to Monsignor Roche. Parents were not convinced that their daughters could not qualify for a girls' national secondary school. The diocese had many primary schools, among them, primary schools for girls only, like Nkhamenya Girls Primary School, Katete Boarding Primary School, Lunyangwa Girls, St Maria Gorretti, St. Mary's and Kaseye. Many parents thought that the diocese had better knowledge of what was going on and could provide a solution.[83]

Female Students at Mzuzu Technical School

In the late 1980's, the government decided to put female students at Mzuzu Technical College which was primarily for males. Monsignor Roche felt that the decision was good but requested if it could delay until girls' hostels were built. However, the decision was enforced without consideration of his request as an agent of the school. With Marymount a few metres away from the technical school, he felt that a similar decision could be enforced on Marymount to become a mixed school.[84] He felt that as proprietor of all grant-aided schools in the diocese, he had less and less control in the administration of the schools.

Relocation of Teachers to their Place of Origins

The 1989 saga of expulsion of teachers to teach in their own regions troubled Monsignor Roche.[85] Both primary and secondary schools in the north had an influx of teachers but without proper accommodation. As a result, many teachers thought of getting early retirement or change jobs. Monsignor Roche felt that he had a role to play as a spiritual father of those who had lost zeal for the teaching profession and whose future was depressive. Generally, the quality of education in the country started to deteriorate with this drastic move. The youth started to dislike the teaching profession especially if their parents or relatives had been victims of the situation. The climax came about within the first ten years of multiparty democracy where, with the gap in the teaching profession, government employed over 22,000 untrained

---

[83] Interview with Mr M. Phiri, a parent in Mzimba, on 27.7.2010.

[84] Interview with Sr Huguette Pigeon, MIC, Mzimba, 31.7.2010.

[85] Angela Hanley, *Justified by Faith. St Patrick's Missionary Society*, Kiltegan: Wicklow, p. 93.

primary school teachers.[86] This had consequences on academic performance as well as on the moral and social relationships of learners who left primary schools for secondary school education. For Monsignor Roche, a private secondary school was the best solution and a well-qualified and experienced human resource was at his disposal.

The Lenten Pastoral Letter of April 1992: "Living Our Faith."

The aftermath of the release of the Lenten Pastoral letter of the Catholic Bishops in 1992, saw the untimely expulsion of Monsignor Roche from Mzuzu Diocese, and from Malawi as a whole.[87] Marymount was to become private in September 1992, and it did so, in his absence.

A Rebirth of Marymount

The unique event in the whole transition of Marymount happened on 1st September 1992 when the school opened with new staff and students. The school started with forms one and three. It was advertised in the newspapers of June 6, 1992 on the last day of graduation as a grant-aided institution.[88] Teachers and students of form 2 and 4 were posted to other national schools before the beginning of the new academic year. Many girls were posted to mixed schools and found the changes painful because in some schools, their performance was affected drastically and negatively.[89]

The Objectives for Privatization

On 28th June 1993, the Acting Apostolic Administrator, Monsignor Joseph Mukasa Zuza, visited the school. He held meetings with the

---

[86] Ministry of Education, Sports and Culture, Education Sector, PIF Document, June 2000, p. 3.

[87] MIC Chronicles, 6.6.1992. On that occasion 81 students graduated. Amongst the invited guests were the Vicar General, and Mrs L.C. Chihana.

[88] His letter of deportation was delivered to him on Good Friday whilst conducting the liturgy of the day. This event better integrates his experiences in Malawi as a man "justified by faith." This is the title of a book by Angela Hanley depicting the missionary experience of Monsignor Roche, dedicated to "all those who speak the truth and are willing to suffer the consequences."

[89] Interview with Caroline Msukwa, who experienced this change on 5.9. at Montfort Campus.

students and staff. Towards the end of the year, Monsignor Roche returned to Mzuzu, and assumed his role as Administrator of the diocese. On 4th of February, 1994, he visited Marymount and celebrated a Thanksgiving Mass in the school chapel. It is during this first visit in its privatized status, that he reiterated his dream for the school. Addressing his audience, Monsignor Roche said; "My dream of the privatization of Marymount is no longer a dream. It has come to birth through you ...

Bishop Joseph Zuza

I thank God for the varied gifts he has gifted you with!"[90] The Constitution of Marymount Catholic Secondary School stipulates six objectives for the privatization of the school.[91] It mentions provision of quality education for Catholic girls in Malawi, preparing them for leadership roles in the Family, Church and State.

Another focus is on the provision of a more wholistic approach to education by ensuring the formation of faith and humanities for Catholic Girls. It further states the creation of an atmosphere where students will grow in body and spirit as well as in maturity, responsibility and in true respect for each other. The last three objectives mention the provision of opportunities for students to broaden their horizons in spiritual, intellectual, emotional, physical and social life. Furthermore, to provide opportunities for students who would otherwise not have the chance to pursue Secondary School Education and finally, to provide financial sustainability for Mzuzu Diocese through school fees and other income generating activities at the school.

Role of the Church: Mzuzu Diocese

As proprietor of the school, Bishop Joseph Zuza entrusted the running of the school to the Board of Governors. His role remains to ensure that the school is run according to Catholic ethos and the standards set by

---

[90] MIC Chronicles, 4.2.1994.

[91] Constitution of Marymount Catholic Secondary School. 3.0, Fundamental Objectives 3.1-6.

the Ministry of Education, Science and Technology (MOEST).[92] The education commission in the diocese also facilitates the advancement of quality education. It actively participates in various educational groupings and associations that aim at improving the quality of education. For instance, it is a member of the Association of Christian Educators in Malawi (ACEM), which is an ecumenical body under the Malawi Council of Churches (MCC) and the Episcopal Conference of Malawi (ECM). The mission of the association is to develop, establish and promote a quality and wholistic educational system that adequately caters for the whole person as made in God's image. ACEM was formed in 1994 as a response to the challenges ensued by the Free Primary Education (FPE) Policy.[93] It implies that the Church at local and national level supports government's efforts in the promotion of education, and girl child education in particular.[94]

Role of MIC Sisters

The dream of Monsignor Roche to transform Marymount into a Private Catholic Secondary School was communicated to Sister Suzanne Leclair, the Programmevincial Superior of the MIC Sisters at the time. With her council, they held a meeting on 27th of April 1991, to discuss their new

International group of MIC sisters during a provincial meeting

role in the running of the school. The Sisters welcomed the idea of privatization of Marymount with mixed feelings. Some among them accepted it wholeheartedly as a relief because they did not have enough personnel to ran the school as before. Others regretted the move thinking that the school would only favour the rich families and deny the poor masses quality education. Besides, it felt to them like losing control of the school in which they had invested a great deal of

---

[92] Interview with Monsignor Muwowo, Vicar General of Mzuzu Diocese on 31.7.2010.

[93] ACEM, vol 3.1, p. 4.

[94] Interview with Mr Mastara, National Educational Secretary, Episcopal Conference of Malawi (ECM), headquarters in Lilongwe, 22.7.2010.

resources. Eventually, the Sisters accepted to contribute personnel for the school according to their provincial priorities. These included teaching and taking care of the spiritual needs of students at Marymount and other schools within Mzuzu.

Role of the Government

The government has the responsibility to ensure quality education for its citizens. The Ministry of Education registers schools or de-registers schools that lack conducive environment for teaching and learning. It also ensures curriculum implementation and professional growth of teachers. In private schools, government expects that 50% of teachers are competent, with diplomas in education or higher qualifications. It expects private schools to invite inspectors for seminars on school management, methodology and assessment. In-Service Training (INSET) is also encouraged.

The Ministry also involves private schools in subject orientation during examinations and incorporates them in the cluster systems where some schools like Marymount continue to be examination centres. The government registered Marymount as a Catholic Private Secondary School, but with mixed reactions from some of its officials. Some challenges included re-allocation of teachers and students, as well as loss of resources.[95]

Re-allocation of Teachers and Students

The privatization of Marymount reduced the number of places for selection to form one. The school was one of the best national girls' secondary schools. There was over-enrolment in government schools of both teachers and students. Marymount had close to sixteen teachers and about 360 students, of whom 279 had to be re-allocated to other schools.[96] There was an oversupply of teachers within secondary schools in Mzuzu who could have been useful somewhere else. The issue was that some female teachers could not be posted outside the city leaving their spouses behind in other sections of the civil service or

---

[95] Interview with Mr Luhanga and Mr Soko, EMAS Regional Offices in Mzuzu, 26.7.2010.
[96] About 81 students graduated from Marymount in 1992, it meant that the rest had to be re-allocated without considering new recruits.

private sector. According to some ministry officials, these postings were not procedural but like an emergency.[97]

Loss of Equipment

In the process of privatization, there is loss of equipment and difficulties of accountability from both government and new proprietors.[98] Some inventories do not specify ownership of certain facilities like text books, other teaching and learning materials and infrastructure. In some instances, buildings like hostels can be looked at as a loss from the side of the government.

By privatizing Marymount, the relationship with government was shaken.[99] However, both the Church and government respondents did not have any records of removal of any material resources from Marymount. Actually, Church authorities intervened, and the issue was sorted out amicably, but government developed some anxieties to invest in any grant-aided institution, especially belonging to the Catholic Church, for fear of having them privatized. Government tends to think that such investment would turn into a commercial entity.[100]

Church-State Relationship on Educational Matters

Through this study, it is established that at times there is friction between Church and State on educational matters. This cold war is detrimental to the well-being of citizens. The role of the Church is an asset to the State whose primary responsibility is to educate its citizens and provide adequate resources to that end. By offering education, Churches are fulfilling their mission of saving both the body and the soul of human beings without being partisan to the government of the day. On the other hand, there is misinterpretation of such roles which dents the image of partnership that exists between Church and State. According to the educational history of Malawi, many prominent people in the civil service and the private sector have passed through mission schools. Ultimately, it is the government that remains the primary beneficiary of development through quality education of its

---

[97] Interview with Mr Luhanda, Mzuzu.

[98] Interview with Mr Luhanga, EMAS Offices, Mzuzu.

[99] Interview with Mr Mastara, National Education Secretary at the Episcopal Conference of Malawi (ECM), 22.7.2010.

[100] Ibid.

workforce received from grant-aided institutions, run by Churches and other private entities.

Advantages of Privatization

Increase in Enrolment

As a private institution, enrolment has doubled, offering access to more girls to attain quality education at a reasonable fee.[101] Before privatization, an average of 82 girls per year completed their form four at Marymount. Since privatization, over 165 girls complete their secondary studies at the school. Before that, the Ministry of Education was responsible for selection of students. The enrolment of Catholic girls was minimal. This was detrimental to the preservation of Church, culture and doctrine. Catholic girls are custodians of Catholic teachings and faith to later generations and for the growth and support of the Church.[102]

Single Sex Education Policy

Privatization enhanced the single-sex education policy enforced by the Catholic Church in its education framework. This has allowed more girls to attain secondary education of good quality. The diocese felt the need to establish a model school in academic performance and character formation. Likewise, it was easy for the Board of Governors to implement its own policies that benefited the Church as well as the State without infringing on the right to education of all people.

Source of Employment

The board has a right to choose and employ quality teachers and support staff dedicated to their work. The loyalty of teachers to the proprietor and the school is not divided as it is in a grant aided institution.[103] Many teachers at Marymount have taught in other schools and retired and yet find fulfilment in teaching. A blend of experienced and young teachers is another healthy secret for the success of the

---

[101] Interview with the Dicoesan Education Secretay for Mzuzu Diocese, Mr J.S.C. Longwe, Katoto, Mzuzu, 30.7.2010.

[102] Interview with Monsignor Muwowo, Katoto, Mzuzu, on 31.7.2010.

[103] Interview with Mr Mastara, 22.7.2010.

61

school.[104] Whilst private schools strive to retain quality teachers, Marymount has an influx of applications from both teachers and students and yet it does not place adverts in newspapers for recruitment and enrolment of students. The good results of the school advertise for themselves.

Source of Income for the Diocese

The school has become a good means of income for the Diocese of Mzuzu as perceived by Monsignor Roche, who felt that it needed a steady means of generating funds, whilst at the same time, offering viable services. The school had to ensure that it keeps to its identity as a Christian institution and avoid the temptation of focusing on profit-making. It is appreciable that the needy students are helped through bursaries. The Board of Governors allows that the school sponsors three students, one from each deanery every year.[105] In addition, existing developmental projects have been enhanced and new ones initiated as income generating activities to supplement the fees.

Challenges

The major challenge that the school encountered was a strike by students that merited them expulsion from school in March 1996. It was the first time in thirty-three years to have such a strike which forced the proprietor and board of governors to close the school one month earlier than calendared. The Board had dismissed its head teacher due to some administrative irregularities on his part. However, the information reached the students in a distorted manner as it was impossible to give the reasons because of discretion and respect for the head teacher.

Sr. Yvonne Ayotte was the Chairperson of the Board at the time and she was faced with rude coldness and the information she gave received no credence.[106] The incident was vividly explained in this way:

---

[104] Interview with the current head teacher, Mr JJ.R. Banda, 31.7.2010.

[105] Interview with Mr J.S.C. Longwe, T.D.C. Gondwe and the chairperson of the Board of Governors, Sr Huguette Ostiguy, MIC, on 29.7.2010. From 2.11.2010, Mzuzu Diocese was divided into two, thus Mzuzu and Karonga Dioceses. The three deaneries incorporated the newly established Diocese of Karonga. The data in this research covers the jurisdiction of Mzuzu Diocese before this change.

[106] MIC Chronicles, 25.3.1996.

that after the emergency Assembly, the students, instead of going to their classes, nervously decided to organize themselves, Form 4's being on the lead. Marked displeasure is written on their faces. The school bell is rung undisruptively. Unbecoming words are uttered within hearing. A red piece of cloth is hoisted on the flagpole. And then, in mob-like mood and in willful disregard of the out-of-bounds rule of the school, the students walk out of the school campus ... to town and on to the Bishop's House in Katoto. The observed defiant behaviour of the students overwhelms the staff ... The sun has set. The Deputy Headmistress and most of the teachers are huddled in the staff room, wondering, reflecting, pondering. An hour or so later, students arrive. In the dark some dare speak loud their bad intent to vandalize the tuckshop, the lab rooms and the Home Economics building. Wishing to put order into the situation, the Deputy Headmistress and Form Masters ask for a roll call and they invite the students from the hostels to the classrooms. But the students would not obey and they threaten the teachers.[107]

Apparently, the students walked about 10 kms from Marymount to the Bishop's house in Katoto. Eventually, over 152 students were still out at Katoto by 11:40 p.m. while Sisters Yvonne Ayotte and Bibiana Flora were with the teachers in the staff room. The students were transported back to Marymount in five trips around 2:30 a.m. Early morning, all students had to leave for their homes. The parents were informed in a radio broadcast, and students who wished to come back had to re-apply. This type of behaviour reflected the mood of Malawi in its young democracy. Many students in the early years of multi-party democracy took to riots and strikes as solutions to their grievances. Such incidents showed that the new democratic era had impact in all spheres of life and was visibly pronounced in educational institutions.

Conclusion

This chapter has focused on the transition period of Marymount from a grant-aided institution to a private Catholic Secondary School in 1992. It has further discussed the major roles of the Church, MIC Sisters and the Government in that process. The major advantages and challenges that the school experienced in the early years of its privatized status have also been explained. The next chapter will concentrate on the growth of Marymount from the year 2000 to 2010.

---

[107] Ibid.

Chapter Five
Marymount 2000 - 2010

The fruits of the transitional process started to be clear after the year 2000. This chapter will focus on Marymount from 2000-2010. It will stress on the involvement of MIC Sisters and the general organization of the school as it continues to progress.

MIC Sisters' Involvement

Teaching and Support Staff

The number of MIC Sisters started to decrease in this period. Replacements were very sporadic and the same persons would assume various responsibilities at the school as well as in the running of their congregation. For instance, Sr. Yvonne

Sr. Rosetti Lau MIC with her class

Sr. Catherine Wan and Leontine Lang inside MM chapel

Ayotte, was Chairperson of the Board of Governors, and replaced two accountants at the school. She was also Youth Coordinator of the Diocese and assumed various other responsibilities in the community. Sr. Yolanda Oducado moved from St. John Bosco Secondary School at Katete, to teach at Marymount. She became deputy headmistress in 1998, but moved out towards the end of 2000, as she was elected Provincial Superior of the Sisters.

Other Sisters at Marymount included Sr. Rosetti Lau as a Biology and Bible Knowledge teacher. Sr. Jacintha Henry, a student with the Catholic University of East Africa (CUEA) in Nairobi, came for teaching practice. After her graduation, she was appointed to the MIC school in Hong-Kong as first MIC African Sister to that part of Asia.[108] Earlier on, Sr. Catherine Wan from Hong Kong was at Marymount and worked for youth animation and was instrumental in the renovation and for the beautiful art work in the Chapel. She worked together with Sr. Leontine Lang. Sisters Hélène Gemme and Marie Leclair worked as librarians at the school.[109]

Youth Alive Malawi

Sr. Yvonne Ayotte started the 'Youth Alive Mzuzu' in 2000 to sensitize the youths on HIV and AIDS issues. The movement grew fast and soon changed its name to Youth Alive Malawi, due to its wide coverage of programmes. Various training sessions for both boys and girls were initiated within and outside the country. Youth Alive groups were formed in most secondary schools where the Sisters went for such seminars.

Sr. Threazer Banda with students

Young Christian Students

The Sisters also continued with their active involvement in YCS. During the annual Diocesan Council meeting held at Marymount in 2005, 85 students from 36 secondary schools attended. The two-day session was preceded by a retreat organized by Sr. Yvonne, and the Marymount Chaplain, Fr. Jim McGuire. Much of the activities in YCS

---

[108] Whilst working in Malawi, the Sisters are also in solidarity with fellow missionaries in other countries and the readiness to assist where need be, is fundamental for a missionary family spirit. Although few in number, African Sisters are trained to also look beyond the needs of their local church.

[109] A few years later, the two Sisters retired, after having worked for many years.

are integrated with activities of Youth Alive Malawi. This is because, 'Youth Alive,' though a social group in nature, is founded on moral, religious and spiritual values. Training of youth leaders was emphasized and Marymount students became first trainers of fellow youths in Mzuzu and other secondary schools in Malawi.

Form Four Performance 2000 – 2010

Year	Number entered	Number passed	Pass rate	University selection
2000	127	76	60%	22
2001	120	87	73%	21
2002	135	120	87%	52
2003	138	133	96.4%	**62**
2004	162	149	92%	55
2005	152	140	92%	65
2006	159	151	95%	54
2007	168	156	92%	48
2008	162	160	99%	69
2009	164	162	98.7%	93
2010	168	167	99.4%	-
	1655	1501		541

The 40th Anniversary of the School

In September 2003, Marymount celebrated the graduation of 140 students as well as 40 years of foundation as a school. On this memorable day, Bishop Zuza officiated at the solemn Mass. Sr. Yvonne Ayotte gave a brief history of Marymount. The year 2003 was unique as well in terms of academic excellence. The table above records the form four academic performance of Marymount from 2000 to 2010.[110]

Since privatization in 1992, the school experienced the highest pass rate for form four examinations as well as for university selection in 2003. The school recorded a 96.4% pass rate with 62 girls for university selection. These results have continued to improve and show that more than half of those who pass their form four proceed to institutions of

---

[110] The records were provided to me by Mr J.R. Banda, head teacher at Marymount July – November 2010.

higher learning. It is to be noted that the university selection counts the constituent colleges of the University of Malawi only, except in 2009 which had 67 students for the University of Malawi (UNIMA), and 26, for the University of Mzuzu (MZUNI). The 2010 results were the most impressive since the academic session was very short due to changes in the academic calendar.[111]

School Awards

Marymount has received numerous awards within the past ten years. On the academic level, the prominent awards are from the National Commission for Science and Technology. The school received the second best female science school award in 2006 from the National Research Council of Malawi. In 2009, it received a similar award from the National Commission for Science and Technology. In the 2009-2010 academic year, the school emerged the best in the female students category. In July 2010, Marymount emerged on position seven in the National Science Fair at Kamuzu Academy having improved from position 17 the year before. In the arts and sportive activities, the school keeps improving in many aspects. For instance, in 2008 Marymount came first in the 24th Festival of French Drama. It maintained the position the following year. In sports, the school received the Ladies Category Table Tennis award in 2009.

---

[111] Interview with Mr J.R. Banda, on 19.11.2010 at Marymount. The government reversed the academic calendar so that all schools begin in September. This reduced the academic weeks to about 36 instead of 39 weeks. According to the head teacher's remarks, he stated that at Marymount, the teachers themselves requested to teach 12 periods instead of the usual 9 periods. They also taught on Saturdays. In that way, they were able to cover the entire syllabus and had enough time for revision. The success is attributed to this arrangement, which they shared with other neighbouring schools. However, it demanded commitment of both learners and teachers. The university selection for 2010 is not recorded, as this data was recorded few days after release of the examination results.

Other achievement awards came from The Malawi Writers' Union, The People's Project Citizen Malawi under the Domasi College Civic Education Programme, and also from Zodiak Broadcasting Station for its participation in the women's desk Secondary Schools Girls

Some MM awards in the headteacher's

Literary Competition. Zodiak, a privately-owned radio station, also initiates sponsorship for the girls who emerge with six points in secondary schools. In 2010, two Marymount girls were awarded scholarships to China by the initiative of Zodiak. This shows the vital role of the media in advocating for quality education besides entertaining and informing the public on various issues. It has the capacity to influence other stakeholders to play an active role in the promotion of girl child education in Malawi.

Human and Material Development of the School

According to the current Board Chairperson, Sr. Huguette Ostiguy, staff development activities are intensified for the benefit of both the teachers and the students.[112] The head teacher agreed with this trend. He stated that money is set aside for the training of staff on anything new that arises in the education system. This is budgeted for every year and the school does not wait for government's initiative to organize seminars. Instead, it takes the first step to invite resource persons. In July 2010 revealed that Marymount had 62 employees.

---

[112] Interview with Sr Huguette Ostiguy, 30.7, Marymount.

Table 2. Number of employees

Section	Females	Males	Total
Administration	2	4	6
Teaching staff	6	20	26
Accounts	0	3	3
Librarian	1	0	1
Development	0	4	4
Maintenance	0	3	3
Cleaners	4	0	4
Security	3	6	9
Cooks	0	6	6
	16	46	62

The school has two drivers who are counted as part of the administration. It also recruits casual workers for maintenance on daily basis, and for cleaning on occasions, especially during the rainy season. The security personnel at the school gate have both day and night shifts. The section for development is entrusted with various projects to generate income for the school.[113]

The teaching staff comprises 40% of the work force at the school. The head teacher and two deputies are also part of the teaching staff but are counted under administration. One deputy is responsible for academic operations and the other looks into administrative operations. Privatization of Marymount has allowed the board of governors to expand and employ more teachers to meet the growing demand. It was also discovered that there are more male teachers than females. This is a reverse of what was the norm at the foundation of the school, where the number of female staff was higher as the Sisters were in the majority.[114]

Teachers have a variety of responsibilities and Marymount ensures that they also maximize their potential in other fields apart from teaching in class. For instance, Ms Francine Mwale heads the Development Office responsible for Income Generating Activities (IGAs). The school has a

---

[113] Interview with current head teacher, Mr. J.R. Banda.

[114] In 2010, there was no MIC Sister teaching at Marymount. The only Sister directly linked with the school is the chairperson of the Board of Governors.

piggery with over 28 pigs, about 300 chickens, one cow for milk, a vegetable and maize garden, a banana plantation, a tuckshop and a pay-phone. It also has four big fish ponds for fish-farming. Students who take agriculture have a portion of their own where they do their prac-

Cows for income generating activities

ticals. They cultivate green peas and maize. Upon harvest, the money remains for their club.[115]

Teacher-Pupil Relationship

The seven staff members who were interviewed stated that they were happy to teach at Marymount. Some teachers declared that Marymount is unique as compared to what they experienced in other schools. They were referring to the fact that teaching is not much of a problem because the students have a hard-working spirit.[116] Individual help is offered to those with problems in particular subjects. On the issue of Special Needs Education (SNE), some teachers said that the school does not have learners with special needs. However, three other teachers stated that Marymount has a small number of learners with special educational needs. There is one student identified with hearing problems and she was assisted with hearing aids from Embangweni School for the Deaf.[117]

However, learners who require special educational help are not only the slow learners but also the gifted and talented. Others include students with variable emotional reactions. It was evident in some of the teachers' responses that the issue of special needs education is a new phenomenon. This requires that teachers are provided with information and relevant skills to deal with diverse learners with special educational

---

[115] Interview with Francine Mwale, Marymount, 31.7.2010. Francine took me to visit their gardens, animals, chicken and fish ponds.

[116] Interview with Mrs E.N. Nyirenda, teacher, 31.7.2010.

[117] Interview with Mrs M.R. Nyirenda, 30.7.2010.

needs. This is meant to ensure that people with disabilities are empowered and the best way to empower them is through education.[118]

Major challenges

The teachers outlined some challenges in relation to the school, the students, as well as their relationship with parents and guardians of students. Similarly, the students themselves also spelt out their challenges.

The School

Some teachers felt that the triple stream reduces the number of assignments to give the learners. The librarian also claimed that it is a lot of work for one person. She admitted that the prefects are of great assistance but she cannot depend much on them since they too need to study.[119] One learner felt that the new system of exposing the students' results on the notice board was not to her liking. According to her, "it is so discouraging because there is no way you can make a student improve when you make her a laughing stock."[120] The biggest challenge to the school is in the infrastructure.[121] There is need for renovation of hostels and the building of new ones to reduce congestion. Also, the dining hall is not spacious enough to cater for larger groups at every meal.

The Students

Immaturity

Teachers felt that some girls come at a tender age for secondary school education. Every year in form one; there are small girls of 9 or 10 years of age. As such, many of them do not understand what it means to take responsibility and therefore, taking care of surroundings in general is difficult. One former teacher, who is also an ex-student of the school, had the same sentiment. She stated that,

---

[118] A.A. Ponje, "Where is Malawi on Special Needs Education?", *Sunday Times*, 30.5.2010, p. 5.

[119] Interview with Ms Leslei Paranuik. Leslie is a Canadian lay-Scaboro Missionary.

[120] Respondent.

[121] Interview with Mr J.R. Banda.

although Marymount is generally a clean school, those standards have gone down in the cleanliness of hostels where girls litter everywhere. She further said that they need to be taught basic things like making a bed, since for some; it is their mothers or workers who were responsible for such chores at home. Other teachers felt that although age counts, it is the family upbringing that makes the girls responsible or not on such issues.

Discipline

Issues of going out of bounds are common especially towards the period for examinations. Like in most schools, the period approaching MANEB examinations is a challenge to schools. Also, the different characters of girls become challenging when they fail to adhere to

Time for study at student's corner

school rules and regulations. Peer pressure makes some girls influential leaders when it comes to trouble making. In the evenings, lights are off from 9 p.m. to 3.a.m, but some girls still wish to study in between that time using candles. This not only disturbs others but is very dangerous in a dormitory with many girls.[122] In order to curb such tendency, the school allows one security lady to sleep in the hostel and she is also helpful when a student is sick at night, to notify the appropriate authorities. On their part, the students felt that some teachers are too strict as they come up with too many restrictions.

One respondent said; "I feel the don'ts are more than the do's." On the other hand, another claimed that she does not like it when students do not want to follow the school rules.

Communication

The students are required to communicate in English amongst themselves and with teachers for academic purposes. However, one teacher complained that this regulation is not kept. Instead, Chichewa dominates in their conversations and this deters them from speaking

---

[122] Interview with the boarding mistress, Ms. Francine Mwale, 31.7.2010.

good English. Eventually, it contributes to poor writing skills. Another reality is the use of cell-phones in the hostels. Students at Marymount are prohibited from keeping cell-phones to avoid disturbing others at night and also communicating with people at awkward hours. The school recommends that the phones be surrendered to the deputy head teacher who returns them to the student at the closure of the school.[123]

Dressing

Some girls like to wear short skirts even though they are taught to dress properly with their skirts below the knees. Some even make their own skirts with pockets and the colour slightly different from the blue of Marymount. One teacher stated that he does not encounter much challenges from the students, but he observed that there is competition amongst themselves on status. Some like to show off, if they are from well-to-do families. An ex-student also affirmed that she noted the same experience when she came back to teach at the school. In her time as a student, it was very difficult to notice that gap between the rich and the poor. She used to learn in class with daughters of ministers and relatives of Kamuzu Banda, and yet no one would notice the difference in status.

Relationship between Teachers and Parents

Teachers stated that their relationship with parents is very good. However, two of them mentioned that at times it is less encouraging to them as teachers. On the positive side, the teachers felt that most parents are cooperative and appreciative of the contribution that teachers are making in the lives of their daughters. Parents raise funds for the school and come for open days, graduation and special occasions. Many of them come during the visiting day once a month. Some parents even donate to the school. There was mention of one parent who donated twenty chairs. On the other hand, some parents take the side of their daughters against the school rules especially on discipline and use of cell-phones. The teachers referred to a case where girls in form 4 misbehaved just a month before their examinations. One parent mobilized the other thirteen with only two who refused to be part of the court injunction against the school. Although the school won the case in court, "such incidents do not help the school to instill proper

---

[123] Interview with teacher no. 1, 28.7.2010. On some issues I choose to leave the names anonymous and to identify the respondent by a number.

discipline and maintain good relations with parents."[124] It also trespasses on some of the rights of teachers in their conduct as professionals in their job of fostering discipline in the school.

Relationship between Parents and the School

This study has established that the majority of parents have excellent links with the school. Parents appreciated the fact that teachers send school reports every term which helps them to follow the performance of their daughters and give them

Marymount staff and board members

appropriate assistance in turn. They mentioned that they do their best to attend parents' meetings. Others try to come every month on visiting days and feel that it is an effective monitoring tool for their daughter's welfare and academic progress. One male parent appreciated the fact that he is not aware of any record of sexual abuses of teachers towards girls. He has sent two daughters and three relations at different intervals and teachers have always respected the girls. As such, Marymount continues to be a school of highest integrity in Malawi largely because parents feel secure to entrust their daughters to it, knowing they will be respected at all cost.[125]

School Fees

Amongst the respondents, 10 stated that school fees are a big challenge for them. It is difficult to source it within a few months. At the beginning of the term in September 2010, the fees were at MK 55,500. The study established that many parents who send their daughters to Marymount are middle income workers who manage with meager salaries. Some of them are in the civil service and struggle to find other sources of income for their sustenance. One parent stressed that she makes a lot of sacrifice in the education of her daughter because she has other children and dependents in day schools and institutions of higher learning.

---

[124] Interview with teacher no. 2, 29.7.2010.

[125] Interview with parent no. 4, 24.7.2010, graduation day.

In contrast, two other parents claimed that they find the fees reasonable for a private secondary school with the quality of teachers and the performance it produces. One of them affirmed that; "in a CDSS or government school, our daughter would not do as well as here and we want the best for her."[126] The parent also stressed that the diet is good and teachers need good salaries to motivate them to give their best. Compared to other private boarding secondary schools, she finds that Marymount is one of the cheapest as quality education is invaluable.[127]

It was also observed that there is more involvement from female than male parents in maintaining the link between home and school. The males revealed that they have not been actively involved due to the nature of their jobs and distances. The two males who live in Zomba and Chikhwawa stated that they have never attended Parent-Teacher Association Meetings (PTA) and have had no form of contact with the teachers. One parent observed that he finds the pupil/teacher ratio very high and feels that "a large class does not allow each child to receive attention that makes one feel special."[128] He further explained that the school has many intelligent students and some teachers may not give much attention to those who are struggling and instead utter remarks that demoralize them.[129]

Conclusion

This chapter has focused on the life of Marymount from 2000 to 2010. These ten years give a broad view of the school as it stands and continuesto progress. Having looked at this history, the next chapter will focus on what I think is the contribution of MIC Sisters to girl child education in Malawi.

---

[126] Interview with parent no. 1, 24.7.2010, graduation day.

[127] Interview with Mrs S. Nyirenda, 24.7.2010, on graduation day.

[128] Interview with parent no.1.

[129] Ibid.

Chapter Six:
The Specific Contribution of MIC Sisters to Girl Child Education

The previous chapters have concentrated on the history of Marymount Catholic Secondary School since its inception in 1963. The account has given a glimpse of the educational endeavours that have formed both the unique history of the school as well as that of the girl children who have studied there for the past forty-seven years. This chapter will focus on the contribution of MIC Sisters to girl child education in Malawi. The facts are based on the experiences of the MIC Sisters and former students and how they assess themselves.

School Ethos

Marymount Motto: "Work with Joy"

On arrival at the gate of Marymount, one is struck by the symbol of the school beautifully painted on the wall on the right side of the gate. There is a big "M" sign on a hill and the words "Work with Joy" underneath. The "M" represents Marymount which is built on a plateau. It refers to Mary the Mother of Jesus Christ, who set out at the time as quickly as she could into the hill country to visit her cousin Elizabeth.[1] The encounter between the MIC Sisters and the girls of Malawi is also a meeting of joy that has enhanced a woman to woman empowerment.

---

[1]   Luke 1:39-56.

In 1963, the MIC Sisters through Sr. Doris Twyman designed the motto of Marymount in order to share their Spirituality with the girls.[2] The 'motto' was an excerpt from the words of Delia Tetreault, foundress of MIC Sisters. Delia used to remind her Sisters that *"Work done with joy is never tiresome."* The Sisters believed that study is a form of work and if done with a joyful spirit, one lives not only to enjoy it, but also to benefit from it as her whole being is attuned to living positively, thus creating a power that translates into success.[3]

Solid School Administration

The success of the school is largely dependent on good administration, organization and management of both human and material resources at all levels that touch the board of administration, staff and students. The Sisters ensured proper management of funds and external funding for the school from government, and donor agencies were enhanced due to transparency and accountability of resources. MIC Sisters administered Marymount with some of them as head teachers for twenty (20) consecutive years from 1963 to 1983. After

Sr. Yvonne Ayotte

Sr. Jacqueline Bastien, Sr. Gisele Leduc became head teacher from 1969 to 1973. Sr. Mary Victoria Chirwa took over as acting headmistress until 1976 when she became head teacher until 1979. Sr. Yvonne Ayotte assumed the responsibility until 1983 when a former

---

[2] Spirituality is a way of living one's life that translates the charism or special gift of God to the foundress of a congregation and shared by the members. Delia Tetreault believed that the charism of the MIC is to "spread the Good News of Jesus Christ to those who do not know it in a spirit of thanksgiving."

[3] Sr Doris is also the mastermind behind the design of the cloth (*chitenje*) of the consecrated religious women in Malawi under the Association of Religious Institutes of Malawi (ARIMA) during the General Assembly of the Association of Congress of Women Religious of Eastern and Central Africa (ACWECA), Natural Resources College, Lilongwe, August 2008. ACWECA comprises of Sisters from eight countries, namely Eritrea, Ethiopia, Kenya, Malawi, Sudan, Tanzania and Zambia.

student of Marymount, Matilda Kaluluma (Mrs. Kabuye) picked up headship of the school.[4]

Sr. Yolanda Oducado

Several other Sisters acted as deputy heads for several years such as Sr. Suzanne Rinfret, Leonila Stewart and Marie-Claire Lacombe. The Sisters exposed the school beyond the borders of Malawi with their links with the international community which also formed part of their staff, especially that of lay missionaries. The Sisters' ideas on girl child education became globalized and their views widespread, thus attracting international agents in support of pro-poor initiatives particularly towards the education of the girl child.

After the school was privatized in 1992, Sr. Marie-Claire Lacombe, and Sr. Yolanda Oducado also took their turn as deputy heads.

Leadership Skills

The leadership of the Congregation ensured that the head teachers were Sisters who had good leadership skills and competence in educational matters. The Sisters were not afraid to take risks and learn along the way. The spirit of hard work and dedication instilled by them, laid a solid foundation for Marymount. It is said of the first headmistress Sr. Jacqueline Bastien that the excellent reputation that Marymount has acquired today throughout Malawi is largely due to her spirit of initiative, hard work, and unfailing optimism in the midst of trials and difficulties. In a word, "her truly conquering dynamism!"[5]

Extra-curricular Activities

Extra-curricular activities are vital in the life of any school that aims at wholistic formation of the students. At Marymount, this realization was strongly felt by the Sisters. Through activities, the girls attained a certain sense of exposure in a world that is changing fast. It also

---

[4] Mrs Kabuye is since May 2010 Directress of Finance and Administration in the Ministry of Gender, Children and Community Development at Capital Hill in Lilongwe. She has worked for many years in the Ministry of Education, Science and Technology. From 2001 to 2010, she was in charge of the Inspectorate Section (EMAS).

[5] Sr Gisèle Leduc, Marymount in Retrospect 1963-1973, undated, p. 1.

enhanced a sense of creativity and participation in various programmes which have impact on the student's own career and family life. Extra-curricular activities enrich the personality and ways of doing things due to social interaction. Today's youths are called the 'Facebook or Twitter generation' where they are equally exposed to information through the internet.[6] Much of what attracts the majority of youths are sports, games, music, soap operas and fashion shows that form part and parcel of extra-curricular activities. In the era of the Sisters, a variety of sportive games were encouraged especially in athletics which won the school a place at international games.

Change in Mental Framework

Academic Excellence

At the beginning of the school, all subjects except Chichewa were taught by the Sisters. They were suitably qualified for the subjects they taught. Some of them were trained in Canada before coming to Malawi whilst others went for upgrading in the United Kingdom. In the early 1960s and 1970s, it was a great achievement to have already well-qualified teachers with either a diploma or a first degree in education. This accounts for the good results of the school over the years.

Promotion of Science Subjects

The fact that many subjects were taught by Sisters instilled in the students the self-confidence needed to succeed in difficult subjects such as Science and Mathematics. The tendency to leave science subjects for boys was not felt and girls developed a positive attitude to any subject that was offered.

This was supported by well-equipped laboratories which were started by Sr. Helene Labelle who was then

Mrs. M. Ndovi in the Science Laboratory

---

[6] A BBC radio announcer reporting on the instant links created from various comers of the world by young people accessing the internet to communicate with friends, December 2010.

replaced by Mr. and Mrs. Pawek who were qualified in Physical Science and Biology respectively. Subjects like Physical Science/Chemistry, Biology and Agriculture had each their own laboratory in the first few years of the school's existence. This was also enhanced by a well-equipped library.

Marymount girls perform very well in sciences and this directs their choices for scientific studies in institutions of higher learning. It also fosters the choice of parents who send their daughters to Marymount as they are assured of their girl's excellent performance in science subjects. One former student in the 70s and now working in a bank in Blantyre, wrote; "emphasize on science and technology subjects, economics etc to put girls in non-traditional jobs. Mathematicians, scientists and engineers should come from Marymount."[7]

Role Models

In their teaching, Sisters acted as role-models to the girls. In the early years, many girls who came to Marymount were in their late teens or early to mid-twenties when they started form one. This played a part in their understanding of what was taught and also in the way they discharged their responsibilities. The girls felt that if their fellow women had attained such academic excellence, there was nothing to stop them from attaining the same and even higher grades. One student of the 70s affirmed that: "MIC Sisters were the majority at school and they gave me the impression that they have all attained high education and that as a woman congregation, education was a priority, so I thought, I can also make it in education."[8]

Role Models for Current Students

Government institutions, Non-Governmental Organizations (NGOs), educationists, and some journalists and teachers propagate that female achievers in society, must be invited to schools as role models to girls. There is a strong feeling that girls especially in rural areas fail to

---

[7] Written response to the questionnaire by Bessie Chiunjira. She was at Marymount from 1973-1978.

[8] Interview with Lostina Mtonga (Mrs Chapola), University of Malawi, September 2010. Mrs Chapola is a former student of Marymount and a geologist by profession. She is currently a lecturer in the department of Geography.

complete their secondary school education because they do not encounter fellow women who have excelled in society.

I collected responses of what the girls of Marymount regarded as their role-models at the time of data collection.[9] The request was: "Mention one female Malawian that you admire." The answers were: My mother (9), Joyce Banda (5), Rosemary Mkandawire (3), Anastazia Msosa (2), Jane Ansah (1).

The study has established that the best role models for many girls of Marymount are their own mothers. This reflects the valuable influence that mothers have in the family. Aspects of spirit of hard work, patience, trust and perseverance were outlined as reasons why mothers are admired. One girl wrote; "I admire my mother because she understands me most of the time, she is caring, friendly, and she is the best friend I can trust."[10] Another wrote, "She is a strong believer bringing up 11 children single handedly. I think she is strong."[11] Still,

another said; "my mother worked so hard and she went to college to become who she is right now and she is always working hard to go to a higher level."[12] One wrote; "No matter how a situation might seem impossible, she fights on and never gives up, and life goes on. She helps me to be

A mother and her daughters

---

[9] The names were surely influenced by the socio-political situation in the country at this time. Few months after the 2009 Presidential and Parliamentary Elections, Joyce Banda became the first female Vice-President in Malawi (and in Central Africa). Rosemary Mkandawire is the CEO of Toyota Malawi and former student of Marymount. Justice Anastazia Msosa was the chairperson of the Electoral Commission of Malawi since the first multiparty elections, whilst Jane Ansah is the current Attorney General. These are prominent women in the social circles.

[10] Written response by a form four student of Marymount in July 2010.

[11] Written response by a form three student of Marymount in July 2010.

[12] Written response by a form three student of Marymount in July 2010.

strong no matter what and she encourages me to be perseverant just like her."[13]

The girls who mentioned Joyce Banda as their model, felt that she is a strong woman. She stood her grounds during difficult moments when she was sidelined and eventually dismissed from the Democratic Progressive Party (DPP). This was after she helped to campaign vigorously for the party of Professor Bingu wa Mutharika and won the elections as its vice president.

Mrs. Joyce Banda took over from Dr. Bingu wa Mutharika as the first woman president in Malawi.

Former students still send their daughters and grand-daughters to Marymount. This has created a generation of students whose ancestry can be traced from the 1960s. It is therefore clear that girl child education in Malawi can reach greater heights if mothers themselves are literate. The type of education that the Sisters gave to the first girls, who are now mothers and grandmothers themselves, continues to reflect in later generations.

Character Formation

Former students acknowledge the role of MIC Sisters on their behaviour in terms of ethical, moral and spiritual values. The study established that solid formation of character helps girls to be respected, successful and maintain a certain sense of dignity and simplicity. The Sisters believed in what the girls could become and the girls on their part were struck by the simplicity of the Sisters. A former student said: "The Sisters treated us well and at par, what they saw in us was the potential and on how we devoted ourselves."[14] At the time when the Malawian society was not sensitive enough on gender issues, the Sisters already instilled in the girls, a sense of self-respect and dignity of

---

[13] Written response by a form three student of Marymount in July 2010.

[14] Interview with Matilda Kaluluma (Mrs Kabuye), former student of Marymount from 1965-1969, and headmistress from 1983-1986.

persons. This showed that through formal education, a girl child can learn to enrich her personality, transform her own life and contribute acceptable behaviour to society.

Leadership and Discipline

Former students felt that Sisters as teachers enhanced leadership skills in the students. The Sisters; "were building up our future life to be good citizens and leaders of our country."[15] One respondent said; "We are very determined, orderly adult women leading families and offices because of Marymount."[16] It is evident that the lives of the Sisters spoke louder than words.

Clean Environment

Marymount is known to be a well maintained, clean and beautiful school. This tradition has been kept even by current students as one of them in form four said; "Honestly, I like the environment here. It is very good in terms of infrastructure and surroundings compared to other schools I have visited."[17] The Sisters ensured that the surroundings were kept clean and also that the girls wore clean uniforms and looked smart. The same situation was observed around the premises and classrooms where no broken chairs, desks and torn books would linger around unattended.[18] This would mean that a good physical environment that is clean and hygienic is essential for excellence in

Marymount campus

---

[15] Written response to the questionnaire by Jean Juliet Banda, now retired secretary. She was at Marymount from 1963-1966.

[16] Interview with Victoria Lonje, Area 18, Lilongwe, July 2010. She is a former student from 1974-1978.

[17] Written response by a form four student of Marymount in July 2010.

[18] Interview with Deldwe Kacheche (Mrs Katsonga), former student of Marymount from 1983-1987 and teachers at the same school from 2002-2003. She also sent her daughter to Marymount, who is currently pursuing a degree in education with University of Malawi at Chancelor College.

studies. This provides the girls with a healthy learning atmosphere that is free from diseases associated with crowded environments. Besides, 'cleanliness is next to godliness' as the old adage says.

Cultural Transformation

By getting involved in educating the girl child, MIC Sisters enhanced the transformation of a traditional mindset that focused on a girl child as less worthy of formal education than the boy-child. Culturally, she was expected to get married soon after reaching puberty. Such liberation continues to empower women towards self-reliance and contributes meaningfully to the development of the country at all levels as it is known that "educating a woman is educating the entire nation."[19] The education offered at Marymount became a transforming agent of certain cultural aspects in terms of behaviour and way of living associated with initiation rites at all the important stages of human life such as at birth, puberty, marriage and death. This has led to a change of some traditional conceptions.

Understanding of Certain Taboos

The Sisters succeeded through education in helping girls understand some taboos which were physically abusive on women. In the Malawian culture, many girls were not allowed to eat eggs. Every year, the Sister in-charge of boarding, witnessed a group of form one students who refused to eat eggs. In the early 1960s, a lady cook refused to cook eggs for three hundred borders because she did not want to be responsible for their barrenness. This was the belief at the time that a woman, who ate eggs, especially at menstruation, would become barren.[20] Through lessons in domestic sciences, especially on nutrition, the Sisters helped the girls to understand that eggs enhance good nutrition for the body.

---

[19] A popular adage since as a mother, a woman takes care of both boys and girls as they grow up and imparts knowledge to all.

[20] Interview with Sr Doris Twyman, Provincial Superior, Area 10, Lilongwe, July 2010. Shea learnt this from her students and female workers in the early 1960s.

Initiation at Puberty

Literate mothers explain biological changes that take place in their daughter instead of letting her succumb to certain cultural practices which are secretive and abusive of her person.[21] In a time where some cultural practices are denounced as perpetuating the spread of HIV and AIDS, education of the girl child has demonstrated that a certain degree of literacy is helpful to understand what certain practices and customs cannot clarify in plain words. Without formal education, this cultural transformation would not be possible. It has helped to define a girl child as one who is able to integrate good cultural practices with the changing modern life without neglecting her traditional values as a Malawian woman who is proud to be African.[22]

Family Life

Good family life starts with various experiences that girls encounter at school. Boarding life instills a sense of independence on how to manage life without the close supervision of parents. Girls learn to budget their pocket money and make personal decisions regarding their

The Lonje daughters with their mother.
The three are former MM students.

---

[21] Interview with Dekiwe Kacheche, November 2010.

[22] Modern life for the youth is Western culture. Many youths copy Western lifestyle in terms of food, dress, music, language, dances and use of modern means of communication. However, many youths appreciate local foods, music, traditional wear for girls and dances. In fact, the interest to learn traditional dances and vernacular languages ought to be encouraged.

needs. With such education, girls and women are in a better position to raise healthy families.

This affirms the observation that where women are empowered, there is more education, better health care, and less poverty. Many girls agree that early marriages block a happy and meaningful family life that can better be achieved through education. This study has also established that a few former students of the 1960s, 70s and 80s are widows and yet they have been able to support their children and extended families. Their education at Marymount gave them access to college and university studies which earned them good jobs afterwards. "My husband died, and I have educated my children alone. The determination came with my stay at Marymount;"[23] said one former student whilst another said; "my husband is dead but my life goes on because of my start at the hands of the nuns at Marymount."[24]

Human, Spiritual and Christian Formation

The Sisters ensured a formation to good spiritual life regardless of religious affiliation of the girls and staff. The school welcomed students and staff of various faiths and respected their right to worship accordingly. Similarly, the chaplaincy was also open to fellow Christian leaders who came to the school to conduct prayers for their faithful. This contributed to ecumenical and inter-faith encounters among people of different faiths. Many Catholic girls appreciate the deepening of their Catholic faith whilst at Marymount.

Foundation of Youth Alive Malawi

After the privatization of the school, the Sisters invested more time, energy and resources on sessions and workshops in the area of HIV and AIDS awareness amongst the youths. The movement was started in Malawi in 2000, with the initiative of Sr. Yvonne Ayotte. Its programmes promote abstinence before marriage and fidelity once married as the effective response of a Christian youth to the pandemic. The first Youth Alive Movement in secondary schools started at

---

[23] Written response to questionnaire by Beatrice N'goma, former student of Marymount from 1973-1977. She is currently a Judge at the Magistrate Court, Mzimba District.

[24] Written response to questionnaire by Bessie Chiunjira, former student from 1973-1978, and currently working at a bank in Blantyre.

Marymount and was instrumental in the formation of other groups in the Diocese of Mzuzu and in Malawi as a whole.

Involvement in Church Activities

The Sisters committed themselves to teaching Catechism over the weekends to prepare girls for Christian sacraments like Baptism, Eucharist and Confirmation. In the early years of the school's establishment, a few girls got attracted to the Catholic faith and a few baptisms took place in the Marymount Chapel. For some girls, this experience not only deepened their faith, but also their calling to religious life as was the case with Janerose Nkhana who became Catholic whilst at Marymount.[25] Later, she joined the Sisters of the Holy Rosary (SHR) and served as Superior General of the congregation from 1999 to 2005.

Spiritual formation at Marymount prepared the girls to take up an active role in the running of various church groups in their respective denominations. A former student of Marymount, Dr. Muyeriwa served as National Chairperson of the CWO.[26] One former student said; "I am not Catholic, but I see how the nuns helped me to be who I am today in my Church! I am a Church Elder in Livingstonia Synod thanks to Marymount.[27] Former students also take an active part in fundraising activities and support of their Churches both in cash and kind.

Senior Positions in Society

By the end of the 1960s, the Malawian society began to enjoy the fruits of the good work of Marymount students. A good number had become teachers, nurses, technicians and secretaries. The spirit of hard work quickly helped them to rise to various positions well merited because of their background with the Sisters. By 1976, 86 out of 211 students in the first ten years had graduated from the University of Malawi and 13

---

[25] MIC Chronicles, 5.7.1964. Other girls, who were baptized on the same day are Neffie Makata, Rosemary Nyirenda, Ngawo Msukwa, Bedtsie Nkhata and Ivy Phiri.

[26] Her maiden name is Chrissy Bota and had her sister also at Marymount, Nancy Nyanjagha. One MIC Sister said that Chrissy was a CCAP member whilst at Marymount.

[27] Written response to questionnaire by Beatrice N'goma, former student of Marymount from 1973-1977.

from universities abroad.[28] The first female medical doctor in Malawi was Theresa Mbisa, who graduated in 1970 from a university in Canada.[29] She had been a student of the MIC in Karonga. The number of graduates has risen tremendously along the years.

A Variety of Professions

With this study, I discovered that among Marymount students there is a varied range of professionals. Amongst the respondents was a secretary, a registered nurse and midwife, a former headmistress, a judge, a banker, two accountants, an agriculturalist, a university lecturer, two social workers, a divisional manager of a tea estate and a geologist. With such diverse professionals from a small group of respondents, it is likely to find engineers, primary and secondary school teachers, journalists as well as doctors and lawyers amongst current graduates with a Marymount background. Current staff of Marymount confirmed that their former students are scattered in almost all sectors of the civil service throughout Malawi as well as in the business and private sector. Current students of Marymount mention Rosemary Mkandawire amongst their role models. She is another former student of Marymount and current Chief Executive Officer (CEO) of Toyota Malawi.

Mrs. M.R. Nyirenda former MM student now a teacher at Marymount.

In the Church Circles

Several former students at MIC Primary schools such as at Katete and later at Marymount joined Sisterhood. They have ended up as administrators of grant-aided schools and colleges as well as hospitals under the Christian Hospitals Association of Malawi (CHAM). Amongst the serving headmistresses is Sr. Mary G. Kaunda of Nkhamenya Girls'

---

[28] *Precursor*, 1977, p. 10.

[29] MIC Chronicles, 15.7.1970. Upon arrival to Malawi after her studies, she and her husband and son went to visit the Sisters at Marymount.

Secondary School. In the health service, Sr. Gertrude Msowoya is the Sister-in-Charge of Kasantha Hospital in Karonga. In addition, Sr. Ernestina Chirwa is in-charge of the St. Magdalene Centre in Rumphi which takes care of boys and girls with physical disabilities. In this era of the HIV and AIDS pandemic, Sr. Beatrice Chipeta has been involved in the care of orphans at Lusubilo Orphan Care Centre at St. Mary's in Karonga. This work has won great admiration both in Malawi and abroad.[30]

Sr. Mary G. Kaunda, former headmistress of Nkhamenya Girls. She is current superior general of the Sisters of the Holy Rosary

The Foundation of the Sisters of the Holy Rosary

The Sisters of the Holy Rosary regard the MIC Sisters as co-founders with Monsignor St. Denis, in the foundation of their congregation in Mzuzu Diocese.[31] Sisters Margaret Nyirenda, Marcella Simkoko, Denisa Ng'andu, Janerose Nkhana and Maria Rosa Phiri have served as Superior Generals of their congregation. MIC assisted in the religious

Sisters of the Holy Rosary and MIC Sisters at Mount Rosa in Mzuzu

---

[30] Sr Beatrice Chipeta won the Opus Prize of 2010. This is one of the biggest faith based annual humanitarian awards. She won it alongside Fr John Halligan s.j. of Ecuador for people, who have uniquely touched the lives of the marginalized by addressing social problems such as poverty, illiteracy, hunger, disease and injustice. Ful story is found in Christmas Link of Mzuzu Diocese, Newsletter 135, p. 7.

[31] cf. *Come and See*, Golden Jubilee Issue no. 2 of the Sisters of the Holy Rosary; Sr Janerose Nkhana, *A Brief History of the Sisters of the Holy Rosary*, Balaka: Montfort Media, pp. 2-4.

formation as well as formal education in one way or the other, at Kaseye, St. Mary's, Rumphi, Mzambazi, Katete and Marymount. This assistance continues in the pastoral support and warm relations between these two congregations. Such that, when the MIC personnel started to decrease, their convents, apostolic works in schools, parishes and hospitals were handed over to the Sisters of the Holy Rosary. Likewise, the beautiful white habit with a blue sash worn by the Sisters of the Holy Rosary was the first habit of the MIC's, which Delia Tetreault designed from the life of St. Bernadette of Lourdes.[32]

Current Activities of MIC Sisters in Mzuzu Diocese

MIC Sisters are resident at St. Paul's Parish in Mzimba Boma and at Marymount in Mzuzu City. In Mzimba the Sisters help in running various pastoral activities at various levels. The major activity of the Sisters is the running of Delia Kindergarten for orphans which started in 2006 under the direction of Sr. Charity Zimba. The kindergarten was opened as a viable response to the growing number of orphans left under the care of guardians who are elderly themselves, unable to fully fend for the children in terms of physical as well as academic needs.

The kindergarten ensures a wholistic approach to life and uses the Montessori Method of education where the learner is

Son of an expatriate playing together with other children

---

[32] St Bernadette Soubiros of Lourdes in France is believed to have seen the Virgin Mary on 11th February 1817. She later told her audience that the Virgin Mary was wearing a white dress with a blue sash and covered her head with a veil. This lady told Bernadette that her name was "The Immaculate Conception". Lourdes is one of the famous pilgrim cites for both Catholic and non-Catholc believers for the spiritual and physical healings that take place there. It is not simple coincidence that the liturgical calendar celebrates Our Lady of Lourdes as well as "The World Day of the Sick" on this day every year.

trained to discover their own knowledge.[33] In a sense, the Sisters respond actively to the government's programme of *'M'mera Mpoyamba'* which recognizes that the first five years of a child's existence are crucial for the entire life of a human being.[34] The management of the kindergarten also ensure the continuity of academic support of the children for later years in primary and secondary school. The school has also attracted children who are not orphans as well as children of expatriates working at Mzimba. This openness is healthy for children as it closes barriers that exist due to culture, economic, social and religious differences.

At Marymount, the Sisters run Wongani Kindergarten that was built in 2009 behind the Sister's convent on the same premises on which stood the school for European children in 1956. All the MIC kindergartens register both boys and girls. Unlike in Mzimba which opened specifically

Caregivers with children at Wongani Kindergarten.

for orphans, the one in Mzuzu is private and a reasonable amount of fee is asked from parents or guardians. Nevertheless, the Sisters sponsor a few orphans every academic year. The Sisters also work at Marymount Catholic Secondary School where Sr. Huguette Ostiguy is the current chairperson of the Board of Directors. This is a demanding responsibility as she is also lecturer in psycho-social counselling with the St. John of God College. Similarly, the Diocesan Bookshop and Delia Arts and Crafts Centre at St. Peter's Cathedral are under the management of MIC Sisters. Many parishes and institutions in the diocese and elsewhere have benefited from the expertise of the Delia Arts and Crafts Centre which was started by Sr. Leontine Lang.

---

[33] Interview with Sr Charity Zimba, directress of Delia Kindergarten, Mzimba, 30.7.2010.

[34] "M'mera Mpoyamba" is a program that has become very popular where government and NGOs work together to enforce Community Based Orphans Care Centres, where children learn before starting primary school. The children are provided with porridge every day and in some cases, lunch is also provided.

Sr. Jacquelne Bastien (seated far left) with other retired
sisters who worked in Malawi/Zambia just before her death
in March 1998.

Future Activities

In their pastoral and strategic planning, the MIC Sisters desire to
intensify their activities in education, health, accounting, social work,
mass communication and psycho-social counselling. The younger
generation of MIC Sisters is enthusiastic and determined to continue
the good works of their elderly expatriate Sisters who are retiring and
slowly returning to their homelands.[35]

Conclusion

In this chapter, the contribution of the MIC Sisters to girl child
education in Malawi has been explored through their life-style as
religious women as well as in their role as teachers and administrators
of Marymount. Likewise, the lives of former students have revealed the
kind of education they received in the hands of the Sisters that
continues to mark the life of current students. The chapter has also

---

[35] Outside Mzuzu Diocese, the Sisters have also opened a private
kindergarten called 'Thokozani' at Area 10 in Lilongwe. 'Wongani' and
'Thokozani' are Tumbuka and Chichewa words for thanksgiving, thus
transmitting the spirit of gratitude to God, which characterizes the MIC
Congregation. The two words also fit as personal names given to either a boy
or a girl in a family.

described the present involvement of MIC Sisters and their future plans in Mzuzu Diocese. It is clear that although MIC Sisters seem to focus on girl child education, their future plans support quality education of both boys and girls from the grass root level. The work of pioneer MIC Sisters in the establishment of Marymount, offers to the younger generation of Sisters a rich heritage that still demands continuity of mission and purpose of existence in fostering girl child education in Malawi. The next chapter will outline some suggestions and recommendations that emerge from this study.

A younger generation of Malawian/Zambian MIC Sisters

Chapter Seven:
Suggestions and Recommendations

The previous chapters have presented the history of Marymount and the contribution of MIC Sisters towards girl child education in Malawi. This chapter gives a brief summary of the major findings and offers suggestions and recommendations that would assist MIC Sisters as well as other stakeholders in the process of fostering education as a whole and girl child education in particular.

Major Findings

Marymount as an MIC School

MIC Sisters built Marymount Girls Secondary School to promote girl child education in Malawi. Even after its privatization in 1992, many people who have known the Sisters for a long time still think that the school belongs to the Sisters. Since 1948, over 164 MIC Sisters have been associated with the work of evangelization in Malawi which has largely touched on the promotion of girls and women. More than half this number has on one occasion lived and worked at Marymount and hence participated in the promotion of the girl child either directly or indirectly.

Wholistic Formation

The well-documented MIC Chronicles and other records reflect a sense of vision towards wholistic formation that the Sisters had in educating the girl child. The academic, human, spiritual, emotional, moral, cultural and social aspects were well integrated at the beginning of the school. Similarly, a sense of care for the dignity of persons and for the environment is also perceived depicting evangelical value. In the management of the school, issues of justice, transparency and accountability were enforced for the benefit of the girl child.

Impact on Former and Current Students

The education that the girls receive at Marymount marks them for life. Former students are proud of their school under the care of the Sisters and cherish those memories. Due to the lesser presence of MIC Sisters on the staff in recent years, students, staff members and parents know little about the history of the school and of the MIC Sisters in particular.[36]

Suggestions and Recommendations

MIC Sisters

MIC Sisters are commended for the establishment of Marymount and for working tirelessly with the Diocese of Mzuzu, the donor community and the Ministry of Education Science and Technology to maintain quality standards at Marymount. On the other hand, the privatization of Marymount at the time and the handover to the diocese of their institutions was a regrettable but unavoidable venture on the part of the MIC Sisters who had limited personnel to run the institutions in the footsteps of their pioneering Sisters. Apart from the new kindergarten in Mzuzu, the MIC Sisters are left without any corporate ministry that identifies their mission as Religious women in the Diocese. As such, MIC Sisters could consider building either a primary school or a girls' secondary school of their own as proprietors. This could be a viable means of evangelization that ensures continuity of purpose and mission as a whole and especially so for the African members of their congregation who are joining them.

Mzuzu Diocese

Re-invest in Girls' Education

It is observed that no new boarding secondary school has been built in the diocese except Kaseye Girls Secondary School in Chitipa. The school is still in its foundational phases and uses the former house of the priests as boarding quarters for girls. It still lacks adequate infrastructure for effective teaching and learning. Kaseye is a grant

---

[36] Some current students, staff and parents that were interviewed reflected this lack of knowledge about the history of the MIC Sisters in connection with the founding of Marymount.

aided Girls Secondary School under the Diocese of Karonga since November 2010.

On the other hand, Marymount has a long-standing history of academic excellence and receives thousands of applicants every year but cannot accommodate all the successful candidates in form one. With a continued outcry for the promotion of quality education in the country, the Diocese could consider re-investing in girls' education to continue the founding spirit of missionary institutes. With good planning and adequate funding, a chain of Marymount Schools could attract more girls to receive quality education in the country.

Consider a Marymount Day Secondary School

I agree with Action Aid International Malawi and other researchers on girl child education that single sex boarding schools have proven to be the best for girls but school fees tend to be high.[37] As such, day secondary schools are still a source of hope for many low-income families. Although Mzuzu city has several mixed private secondary schools, the girls do not perform well at MSCE.[38] Therefore; new measures could be explored to open a single stream for day scholars at Marymount. Day scholars could benefit from the already existing infrastructure and other resources without compromising the quality of its out-put.

---

[37] Malawi Human Rights Commission (MHCR) and Action Aid International Malawi, *The existence and Implementation of Laws, Policies, and Regulations in Education and How Affect the Girl — Child in Malawi*, Lilongwe: Action Aid International Malawi, 2009, p. 30.

[38] A copy of the Mzuzu City MSCE results of 2007 gives a clear perception of the performance of girls in mixed schools compared to those at Marymount. It appears as an appendix.

	Secondary School	M	F	Registered Total	Passed M	F	Total	Pass %
1.	Mzuzu Government	72	63	135	43	35	78	57.8
2.	Katoto Sec. School	106	114	220	79	56	135	61.4
3.	Luwinga Sec. School	102	80	182	79	45	124	68
4.	Moyale CDSS	39	29	68	5	16	21	30.8
5.	Msongwe CDSS	9	10	19	3	1	4	21.05
6.	Zolozolo CDSS	27	12	39	8	1	9	23
7.	Nkhorongo CDSS	19	19	38	13	3	16	42
8	Lupaso CDSS	64	41	108	27	4	31	28
9.	Chibavi CDSS	58	36	94	15	4	19	20
10.	Masasa CDSS	33	24	57	7	1	8	14
11.	Marymount Catholic PVT		168	168	-	156	156	92.9
12.	Njerenjere PVT	39	34	73	18	4	22	30
13.	Masambiro PVT	100	78	178	64	35	99	55.6
14.	Mzuzu Reform (Prison)	14	5	19	4	1	5	26
15.	Viphya PVT	116	39	155	84	18	102	65.8
16.	Royal PVT	101	85	186	77	14	91	48.9
17.	St. Peters PVT	71	60	131	36	16	51	38.9
18.	Wukani PVT	25	15	40	14	2	16	40
19.	Joel PVT	42	40	82	20	14	34	41.4
20.	Multi Career PVT	31	13	44	11	2	13	29.5
21.	Chimaliro PVT	43	15	58	22	6	28	48.2
22.	Mundeba PVT	49	36	85	19	5	9	28.2
23.	Mulinda PVT	11	17	28	4	5	9	32.1
24.	Target PVT	67	54	121	37	7	44	36.3
25.	Airtime PVT	62	39	101	30	7	37	36.6

Another possibility would be to build a Marymount Day Secondary School in the vicinity of the existing school and involve the participation of the local communities. Under such programme, many families would manage to pay school fees for their children in a quality single sex day secondary school. Consequently, this could significantly respond to one of the fundamental objectives in the Constitution of Marymount which aims at provision of opportunities for students who would otherwise not have the chance of following Secondary School Education.[39] As it stands now, many Malawian girls fail to complete secondary school studies because of high school fees in grant-aided, government and private boarding schools. Compared to other countries, boarding and day secondary schools in Malawi, do not maximize their human and material resources because of low enrolment.[40]

Freedom of Worship in Catholic Schools

Marymount Secondary School respects the freedom of worship of both students and staff. However, some groups of students do not understand the Catholic ethos and may tend to bring in confusions in the school by inserting their own ways and tastes of prayer that do not conform with Catholic education. As observed in

Students during Sunday Mass

various schools, many Catholic students are easy targets of certain forms of Charismatic and Pentecostal movements because of poor understanding of their own faith and Catholic traditions.

In one Catholic school, some students went as far as distributing anti-Catholic leaflets to fellow students which was disturbing for Catholics who felt strangers in their own school. Marymount has had cases where students were sent home on similar grounds. It is a contradiction to wish to enjoy and benefit from any Catholic school because of its academic excellence and discipline and yet castigate the faith on which the institution is

Students at their own time in the Chapel

---

[39] Constitution of Marymount Catholic Secondary School, Fundamental Objectives 3.5.

[40] This observation was made by an African MIC Sister, who went to the Philippines and visited one MIC day school with an enrolment of 3,000 girls from kindergarten to high school within the same campus.

founded. Proprietors should ensure the availability of a reasonable number of Catholic teachers who could also be dedicated to offer religious instruction and other forms of spiritual help to the girls wherever possible.

More importantly, proprietors and agents of Catholic Schools must clearly establish their theory of a 'Catholic School.' Freedom of worship in schools is a much-talked issue granting that there is an upsurge of Charismatic and Pentecostal groups which target the youths. This is a predicament which calls for joint solutions in the Catholic Church in Malawi after establishing what is meant by 'Catholic School'. Otherwise, what is called a Catholic School, may simply be a name but in practice, not different from any public school with good academic credence.

Employ Full Time Psycho-Social Counsellors

In this time of HIV and AIDS, rampant abuses, sexual harassments and family problems in society, many girls carry within them deep emotional sufferings that infringe on their class participation and academic performance. Regularly, teachers counsel students but this is not ideal because of the conflicting roles that they embrace as educators, disciplinarians as well as parents at one point. Students need emotional support and an interaction at a personal level with someone who can listen to them and offer appropriate advice and skills to deal with their challenges. The Diocese of Mzuzu is privileged to have the services of St. John of God College of Health Sciences. Amongst the Centre's activities are training courses in counselling to promote quality mental health. As such, the Diocese could explore such possibilities and employ full time counsellors for such a noble service to compliment efforts towards academic excellence and character formation of students.

Special Needs Education (SNE)

The Diocese of Mzuzu is also commended for its efforts in the education of learners with disabilities in some of its institutions, especially at St. Maria-Gorretti in Nkhatabay and St. Magdalene in Rumphi. However, serious efforts are needed to ensure that the girls in such institutions complete their secondary school. It is observed that Special Needs Education initiatives are weak in the Diocese of Mzuzu as compared with some of its sister dioceses within the country. As a result, learners with disabilities who also have equal rights to quality education, tend to be forgotten. At times their only hope are fellow compassionate students who do the work for them.

Marymount Secondary School

Emphasize Manual Work and Extra-CurricularActivities

Marymount is a beautiful school. The school must encourage quality time for manual work for the girls and instil a sense of pride in sustaining a clean environment. Similarly, extracurricular activities must be encouraged for all students. The school has kept many of its activities and done well. The Writers Club is applauded for sustaining the production of the 'Echo' magazine which promotes creativity and writing skills in students. The magazine could also incorporate brief articles on former students and staff of Marymount. With internet facilities available in the school, such connections are a possibility that would link up former and current students and staff. Current students would discover their predecessors and learn from their successes in society which could in turn, encourage them to achieve their own dreams.

Involve Role-Models at Graduation Day

Mothers are best role-models to their own children as established in this study. Marymount has a long generation of family ties where mothers desire to have their daughters and granddaughters learn at the same school. The school must widen its activities on graduation day where a few mothers who are former students could be inserted in the programme well in advance to give brief talks to the girls. Also, this would strengthen the Parent Teacher Association (PTA) initiatives in the school.

The Government and Non-Governmental Organizations

Accelerate the Process of Grants to Schools

Government is highly praised for its efforts towards education and girl child education in particular. On the other hand, grant-aided institutions are discouraged with the type of funding that trickles to their institutions and often after struggles with ministry officials. Such bureaucracy frustrates most agents because they feel that their schools do not run as per their desired standards and choose to privatize them.

100

In order to curb this tendency, Government must respect and accelerate the flow of its grants to schools.

Provision of Girls' Hostels

It is worth noting that government continues to provide hostel facilities for girls in many Community Day Secondary Schools throughout the country. Government could take deliberate measures to build additional hostels in already existing girls' boarding schools which have the capacity for extension. This could allow schools to maximize the use of already existing resources. Similarly, NGOs and other donors should continue supporting Church-run institutions which have a long-standing tradition of providing quality education to the Malawian society.

Consider Lowering Temporary Employment Permits (TEP) for Missionaries.

In the past, many missionaries came to Malawi to work in schools and hospitals because the employment permits were affordable. In the recent years, Temporary Employment Permits (TEP) have become very expensive for missionary groups. Some missionary bodies have failed to invite their members to assist them in their work. Such fees could be revised accordingly to attract many expatriates whose work is dedicated for the benefit of the Malawian population especially in schools and hospitals.

Former Students

Put in Place a Marymount Alumni Group

Many former students are successful people in society. This study has found out that the school does not have a body for alumni. One former student said that some efforts had been made a few years ago to create one but she is not aware of any progress to that effect. It is time to seriously think of creating Marymount alumni as the school approaches fifty years of its existence. Former students could be instrumental not only for Marymount, but also in supporting fellow women who are in consecrated life with projects that promote the good of the girl child in Malawi.

Sponsor One Girl Child's Education

Educating an individual requires concerted efforts from various sources. A lot of resources have been invested towards girl child education, and yet there are girls who fail to complete secondary school studies because of lack of school fees. One former Marymount student stated that any girl that cannot pay for school fees must be sponsored and this work must not be left in the hands of Churches, government and NGOs, but to individuals as well. She further stated that she knows that 90% of Marymount alumni can afford more than one girl sponsorship.[41]

Conclusion

This study aimed at exploring the contribution of the Missionary Sisters of the Immaculate Conception (MIC Sisters) towards girl child education in Malawi with particular focus on Marymount Secondary School. This contribution to the development of the Diocese of Mzuzu and the Malawian society as a whole cannot be taken for granted. Indeed, the Local Church, government and donor communities are urged to continue showing keen interest, recognize and support women initiatives in whatever way they can. Similarly, women religious congregations must realize their unique role in the Church and in society and involve themselves fully towards the emancipation of fellow women and girls. Although this research largely focused on the girl child, MIC Sisters did not only limit themselves to the welfare of girls and women. Their contribution cannot be exhausted in this study alone, hence the need for further research to fill in the gaps created by this research. The efforts towards the realization of millennium development goals and the promotion of girl child education in Malawi can be accelerated with women being involved in education endeavors from the grass roots level.

---

[41] Interview with Victoria Lonje, former student in the 1970s.

Bibliography

Unpublished

Banda, Oswald Jimmy, The Enhancement of Girls Education in CCAP Synod of Livingstonia, MA module, Mzuzu University, 2008.

Constitution of Marymount Catholic Secondary School.

Kumwenda, Dayire, Saint Theresa Catholic Parish, Katete: Origins. Growth and Development (1938-2005), BA, University of Malawi, 2005.

Manda, Bridget, Impediments to the Girl Child's Realization of the Right to Access Basic Education in Malawi: The Case of Chintheche Area in Nkhata Bay District, MA, Mzuzu University, 2015.

Masiku, B.C., The Establishment and Development of St. Mary's School, History Seminar Paper 1973/74, University of Malawi, Chancellor College.

Mbewe, Mastone, The Contribution of the Marist Brothers towards Education in Malawi from 1946-2004, MA, University of Malawi, 2006.

MIC Chronicles-Marymount Convent, Mzuzu, 1963-2010.

Mlotha, H.M.Z.H., The Problems which the Roman Catholic Missionaries Faced in Running their Schools in the Diocese of Mzuzu from 1951-1975, BEd, University of Malawi, 1988.

Munthali, John S., The Role of the Livingstonia Synod in the Promotion of Girls' Secondary Education, BA, University of Malawi, 2005.

The Constitutions of the Missionary Sisters of the Immaculate Conception, 5.1, 1983.

Published Sources

"Joint Pastoral Letter of the Catholic Bishops of Nyasaland, 20.3.1961. Lessons from History. 'How to Build a Happy Nation'," 1-12, no. 42, Balaka: Montfort, July-August 2003.

Action Aid Malawi, *The Existence and Implementation of Laws, Policies, and Regulations in Education and how they Affect the Girl Child in Malawi*, Lilongwe, undated.

Banda, Hilda, in *Marymount Panorama*, 1973-1974, vol 11, p. 17.

Banda, Kelvin, *A Brief History of Education in Malawi,* Blantyre: Dzuka, 1982.

Barrette, G., *Delia Tetreault and the Canadian Church*, Laval: MIC Mission Press, 1989.

Baur, John, *2000 Years of Christianity in Africa: An African Church History*, Nairobi: Paulines, 1998.

Bennars, G.A., J.E. Otiende & R. Boisvert (eds), *Theory and Practice of Education*, Nairobi: East African Educational, 1994.

Come and See, Golden Jubilee Issue no. 2 of the Sisters of the Holy Rosary

Gwazayani, P., "Promoting Girl's Education through Mothers Groups." *The Nation*, 17.12.2010, p. 17.

Hanley, Angela, Justified by Faith. St Patrick's Missionary Society, Kiltegan: Wicklow, 2002.

How to Build a Happy Nation, Joint Pastoral Letter of the Catholic Bishops of Nyasaland, 20th March, 1961.

John Paul II, Letter to Women. Presented on the Eve of the Fourth World Conference in Beijing: 4th — 15th September 1995, Balaka: Montfort, 1995.

Leduc, Gisèle, *Marymount in Retrospect 1963-1973*, undated.

Malawi Human Rights Commission (MHCR) and Action Aid International Malawi, *The Existence and Implementation of Laws, Policies, and Regulations in Education and How Affect the Girl — Child in Malawi*, Lilongwe: Action Aid International Malawi, 2009.

Mbiti, John, *African Religions and Philosophy,* London: Heinemann, 1970.

MIC Education Team, "How to Evangelize — Through Education": *Precursor,* 75th Anniversary Issue, 1977 (4), 8-11.

MIC Mission News, April-May-June 2004, "Pathways to Life. Light has Dawned", Interview with Rosetti Lau.

MIC Mission News, October-November-December 2000, "Women in Mission."

Mkamanga, E., *Suffering in Silence: Malawi Women's 30 Year Dance with Dr. Banda*, Glasgow: Dudu Nsomba, 2000.

Mtumbuka, Martin, "Catholic Schooling: Responses of Malawian Students, in G. Grace & J.O. Keefe (eds), *International Handbook of Catholic Education: Challenges for School Systems in the 21st Century,* Part Two, 2002, (pp. 585-617), London: Springer.

Mwaungulu, R.T., *Selected Themes in Church Law. Celebrating 25 Years of Priesthood (1984-2009)*, Balaka: Montfort Media, 2009.

Nkhana, Janerose, *A Brief History of the Sisters of the Holy Rosary,* Balaka: Montfort Media.

Nkhokwe, M., "Parents Key to Education MDG", *The Nation, 01.11.2010,* p. 16.

Ponje, A., "Where is Malawi on Special Needs Education?", *Sunday Times,* 30.5.2010.

Sibande, Zeenah, *The Religious Geography of Mzuzu City in Northern Malawi,* Mzuzu: Luviri Press, 2018

Missionary Sisters of the Immaculate Conception who have Served in the Province of Our Lady of Africa by 2018 (Malawi and Zambia)

Name	Nationality
1. Ayotte Yvonne	Canadian
2. Banda Threazer	Malawian
3. Begin Ruth	Canadian
4. Belanger Yvette	Canadian
5. Blais Therese	Canadian
6. Bouchard Claudette	Canadian
7. Brodeur Pauline	Canadian
8. Cadieux Berengere	Canadian
9. Caron Clemence	Canadian
10. Casuault Yvonne	Canadian
11. Champagne Jeanne d'Arc	Canadian
12. Chihana Wezi Cecilia	Zambian
13. Chilumpha Felistus	Malawian
14. Chirwa Mary Victoria	Zambian
15. Cloutier Marguerite	Canadian
16. Cloutier Blanche	Canadian
17. Corriveau Francoise	Canadian
18. Corriveau Jeanne d'Arc	Canadian
19. Delisle Carmelle	Canadian
20. Denis Louise	Canadian
21. Deziel Therese	Canadian
22. Dufour Colette	Canadian
23. Duhamel Denise	Canadian
24. Dumas Marie-Jeanne	Canadian
25. Fanfan Jeanette	Haitian
26. Flora Bibiana	Phillipina
27. Faucher Edith	Canadian
28. Forcier Jeannine	Franco-American
29. Fortin Marie-Jeanne	Canadian

30. Francoise Florisina	Malgache
31. Frechette Noella	Canadian
32. Gagne Elizabeth	Canadian
33. Gagnon Colombe	Canadian
34. Gauthier Lucienne	Canadian
35. Gemme Helen	Canadian
36. Gauvin Laurette	Canadian
37. Gondwe Wezi	Malawian
38. Guerrero Virginia	Phillipina
39. Guay Rita	Canadian
40. Henry Jacintha	Tanzanian
41. Hervieux Yvette	Canadian
42. Katongo Emelda	Zambian
43. Katongo Marie-Therese	Zambian
44. Katongo Mukuka	Zambian
45. La Salle Lucille	Zambian
46. Lachapelle Suzanne	Canadian
47. Lacombe Marie-Claire	Canadian
48. Lamarche Lise	Canadian
49. Landry Monique	Canadian
50. Lang Leontine	Canadian
51. Laporte Marthe	Canadian
52. Laroche Yolande	Canadian
53. Lau Wai Lan Rosetti	Chinese (Hong-Kong)
54. Laurin Celine	Canadian
55. Lebel Antoinette	Canadian
56. Leclair Marie	Canadian
57. Leclair Suzanne	Canadian
58. Leclerc Colette	Canadian
59. Leduc Gisèle	Canadian
60. Lefebvre Louise	Canadian
61. Legault Marguerite	Canadian
62. Madria Emerenciana	Phillipina
63. Manda Anastazia	Malawian

64. Masinda Vilma	Phillipina
65. Mead Adeline	Canadian
66. Mills Alice	Canadian
67. Mkamanga Catherine	Zambian
68. Mkandawire Judith	Malawian
69. Morin Mireille	Canadian
70. Moriyama Yoko	Japanese
71. Morneau Juliette	Canadian
72. Mzumara Cecilia	Malawian
73. Nyalazi Ruth	Zambian
74. O'Neil Evelyn	Canadian
75. Oducado Yolanda	Phillipina
76. Ostiguay Huguette	Canadian
77. Oullet Gemme	Canadian
78. Pana Vivencia	Phillipina
79. Pare' Gertrude	Canadian
80. Perusse Germaine	Canadian
81. Pigeon Huguette	Canadian
82. Poirier Francoise	Canadian
83. Pumani Judith	Malawian
84. Phiri Mirriam	Zambian
85. Phiri Grace	Malawian
86. Raivomanana Rosalie	Malgache
87. Raso Anthea	Phillipina
88. Richer Georgette	Canadian
89. Rinfret Susanne	Canadian
90. Robert Lise	Canadian
91. Roy Pauline	Canadian
92. Saucier Francoise	Canadian
93. Saucier Gabrielle	Canadian
94. Stewart Leonila	Phillipina
95. Sun Ying-Dz Maria Goretti	Chinese
96. Slyvestre Henriette	Canadian
97. Twyman Doris	Canadian

98. Vachet Jacqueline	Canadian
99. Vallée Jeanne	Canadian
100. Wan Ka Lai Catherine	Chinese
101. Williams Pauline	Canadian
102. Zimba Charity	Malawian
103. Zulu Christine	Zambian
104. Banda Spiwe	Zambian
105. Chalira Susan	Malawian
106. Chewa Rachel	Zambian
107. Gumbo Chance	Malawian
108. Gwaza Georgina	Malawian
109. Kamwela Veronica	Malawian
110. Liphale Lucy	Malawian
111. Razafindahy Ravaka	Malgache

Canadians: 69, Zambians 12, Malawians 14, Philippina 8, Chinese 3, Malgache 3, Haitian 1, Tanzanian 1; Total: 111

Printed in the United States
By Bookmasters